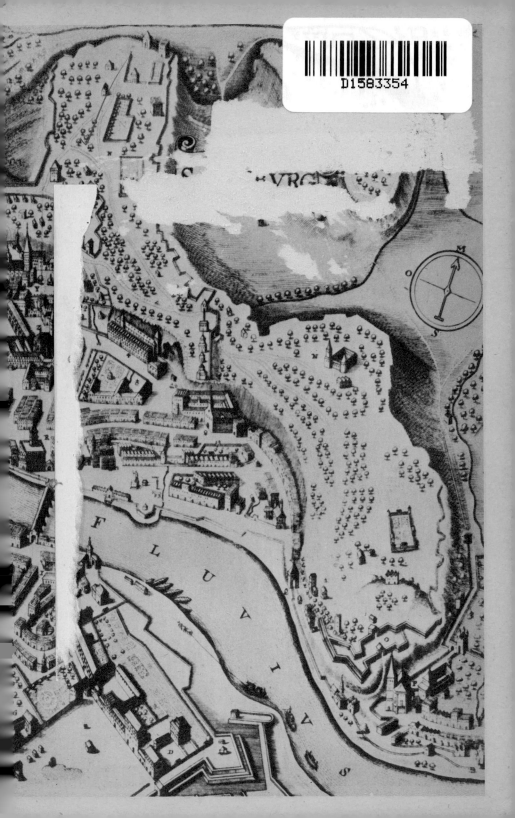

# MOZART IN SALZBURG

By the same Author

HARPSICHORD MUSIC

AMEDEO VOLFANGO MOZARTO SALISBVRGENSI
PVERO DVODENNI
IN ARTE MVSICA LAVDEM OMNEM FIDEMQ. PRAETERGRESSO
EOQ. NOMINE GALLORVM ANGLORVMQ. REGIBVS CARO
PETRVS LVIATVS HOSPITI SVAVISSIMO
EFFIGIEM IN DOMESTICO ODEO P C
ANNO CIƆIƆCCLXX.

MAX KENYON

# Mozart in Salzburg

A Study and Guide

PUTNAM & CO LTD
42 Great Russell Street
London

*First Published* 1952

Printed in Great Britain
by W. & J. Mackay & Co., Ltd., Chatham

DEDICATED
TO
MY COMPANION
AT FUSCHL

# Acknowledgements

The trouble is, in a book of this nature, that so many hares are started, so many people help in the chase, and so many hares finish up by bolting into non-Mozartian holes or thickets. The material collected for this book lies three-quarters unused, and thanks are due to many people.

Many thanks to the Representative in Austria of the British Council, the General Secretary of the Mozart-Gemeinde, the Director of the Carolino Augusteum Museum in Salzburg, the Nationalbibliothek in Vienna, Miss Emily Anderson, M. Alfred Cortot and to Henrietta Vermes for general help and for the loan of illustrations. Many thanks to H.E. the Austrian Ambassador in London for information about the Count Colloredo who held a diplomatic post at the Court of St. James.

MAX KENYON

# Contents

# Illustrations

The letter and numeral references, e.g., " edition of
*Letters* M 19 " are to the Bibliography, pages 204–212.

# Prelude

# LEOPOLD MOZART ARRIVES IN SALZBURG

IN 1736 SALZBURG and the Empire were at peace. Eugene, unique as a successful Austrian general, who helped Maria Theresa to a period of comparative calm, died and his corpse had a magnificent state funeral in Vienna.

In Salzburg the rix-dollar was worth about four shillings and nine pence [A 11], the florin, three shillings and fourpence while the creutzer rated as one halfpenny. Emily Anderson, in her edition of the *Letters* [M 19], takes the creutzer as a little more than a farthing, and deduces that the sixty which go to make up one gulden make two shillings. Taking the creutzer as one halfpenny would make the gulden half a crown. So we may take the gulden at between two shillings and two and sixpence, or between twenty-eight and thirty-five cents.

Leopold Mozart was 16 in 1736, and living in Augsburg. His father, the bookbinder, had just died and the youth's two brothers were already apprenticed to the same trade. But he himself, perhaps because he was the eldest son, had been educated slightly above this station, for hand bookbinding usually meant a small shop and a journeyman or two, with financial rewards no greater than those of a cobbler. Though Augsburg had printing traditions, it was far from being a Venice to support an Aldus. His mother had been his father's second wife : it is tempting to suppose that Anna Maria Gulzer brought a sensitive, musical strain into the Mozart family.

When he was about nine the handsome boy attracted the attention of a priest. Canon Grabner secured him a position in the choir of the Church of the Holy Cross at St. Ulrich. He sang treble, learned to play the organ under Freysinger in a Benedictine Foundation at Wessobrun, and it seemed possible that the boy himself might become a priest.

His widowed mother had his two younger brothers to look after and the Benedictine monks of Wessobrun took increased interest in young Leopold Mozart. How would he like to study theology in the University of Salzburg ?

So Leopold went away from the wealthy Free City of Augsburg, with its mingled Catholics and Protestants, its book printing and binding, through Munich and over the borders of Bavaria, into the Catholic city of Salzburg, with its Italian influences, its music and its University, which taught Law as well as Theology.

The importance of the Archbishop in Salzburg was soon apparent, for soon after Leopold Mozart arrived, there took place the annual celebration of the anniversary of the elevation of Count Paris Lodron to the Archbishopric in 1619. Although over a century ago, this festival in memory of the great diplomat who kept his Province out of the religious wars was celebrated with solemnity every 13th November.

The reigning Archbishop on Leopold's entry was Franz Anton Graf von Harrach. Eberlin was the chief musician in the Archbishop's establishment, and most of the other musicians were Germans. For instance, the violins included J. P. Schorn and J. C. Thuman, both Salzburgians, Nicolaus Meissner, J. G. Vogtenhuber and Joseph Schorn, 'cellists. Only in the name of Caspar Cristelli, a 'cellist, do we have an Italian. Of these musicians, it was Meissner, a bass singer and a fiddler, who became an important friend of Leopold Mozart. Leopold, indeed, the ex-organ pupil, would have listened to Eberlin on the Cathedral organ, and perhaps wondered how best he might secure violin lessons from Schorn or Thuman. Pergolesi, Gluck and C. P. E. Bach were born in the same decade as himself, and though his greater contemporaries never individually affected Leopold's outlook, it is this sort of transitional music which may be looked for in his work, though we will often look in vain, for much of it was composition as he came to be taught it, rather as he himself felt. But his compositions will be dealt with later.

G. F. Lolli was Vice-Kapellmeister, and represented the Italian group, strong, if not yet completely in power. Although a violinist, a sufficient composer and neces-sarily able to take a figured bass on the harpsichord or organ, Lolli no more thought it beneath him to sing tenor occasionally (and tenors in those days were ill considered, applause and consideration going to male sopranos and altos) than Leopold Mozart, when he was Vice-Kapellmeister, thought it undignified to play second violin in amateur gatherings. Whatever intrigues and animosities, scandals and family feuds this narrative may disclose, we may always remember that the Salzburgians were genuine musicians, always able, from time to time, to join together for the sheer pleasure of music making.

We do not need to be more interested in the history of music in Salzburg than were the Mozart father and son, and mercifully for the extent of this Prelude, there was a great deal of history of which they took no notice whatever. Whether, for instance, St. Peter's changed the style of singing and that of the music itself after the Council of Trent, was of no more concern to them than whether Hermann, Monk of Salzburg in the reign of Archbishop Pilgrim II [S 24] was as good a Minnesinger as Oswald von Wolkenstein. Uncompromising modernists, the earliest they needed to look back was to the reign of Wolf Dietrich. His plans for the Cathedral were the ones which were followed, it was he who made the Hornwerk mechanism on the fortress for which Leopold Mozart wrote some music [D 1]. He too founded a Prince-Archbishop's Chapel Royal, or Hofkapelle, and attached to it a school of music, both Leopold Mozart and Michael Haydn doing work there in their time. And in the reign of Wolf Dietrich, too, was started Salzburg printing, Johannes Baumann being the first of the Salzburg series of printers, some of whom later became masters of their craft. The noble laudatory folios with their imaginative engravings in praise of Archbishop after Archbishop never seemed to extend to include any of the Hofkapelle music, and thus Leopold Mozart had to look to Augsburg for his own books and to Leipzig for his son's scores.

As for Opera, Salzburg was never large enough to have a continuous operatic tradition : even such large German free cities as Leipzig only enjoyed Opera intermittently, and Leipzig had no more Opera than Salzburg in the first half of the eighteenth century. As a short way of saying it, Opera here means a regular House giving repertory, opera with a small o means opera of some sort, amateur, travelling company or specially commissioned for a special feast. Salzburg always had opera, but never Opera. When the theatre was at last built it was used by travelling companies and usually for spoken drama with music.

Wolf Dietrich in his time had imported Italian singers, and this Italian influence was waxing as late as the last Prince-Archbishop, Colloredo continually disappointing Leopold Mozart by the replacement of one Italian Kapellmeister by another Italian Kapellmeister.

If by the time of Colloredo Italian influence was at its greatest, and if Wolf Dietrich started this importation of Italians, the suppression of Germanic music was only gradual. Wolf Dietrich had musicians with the names of Funck, Hofhaimer, Peschin, Glanner, Stornius and Gutfreund, though the latter was called " Bonamico," and there was the questionable Tiburtius Massaino. But under his successor there was Steffano Bernardi and Orazio Benevoli.

The close of the seventeenth century saw music established on a regular, even routine, basis. Archbishop Maximilian Gandolphus heard the music of the Mass in the Cathedral, and oratorios sung in various churches, and incidental music to Latin plays in the University. When out of town, in his pleasure palace of Hellbrun, he would be visited by itinerant German or Italian opera companies, and in Muffat and Biber he had two composers of some minor importance.

Muffat was organist of the Cathedral from 1678 until 1690, and his organ works were printed in Salzburg [S 24] instead of the more usual Augsburg. *Apparatus Musico-Organisticus* is more Italianate than German in feeling.

B

Such clichés as that shown in Ex. 1 were used in
Italy as bare contrapuntal outlines and those composers imitating the style of the best Italian Masters
used them too, they being found, indeed, as far north
as Purcell's Westminster.    Whereas the more purely

Ex. 1

German style of organ composition, as exemplified in
Buxtehude, used more involved figurations and counterpoint tended to obscure rather than energise the rhythm,
Muffat's part writing was clear and used in such a way as
to exploit the rhythm to the full.    Essentially it would
seem that what Gandolphus wanted was what England's
Charles II wanted, music with regular metric stresses
made the more obvious by harmonic rhythm disguised
under an apparently contrapuntal texture, to which the
monarch could nod if the tempo was slow, and tap with
his foot if the tempo was fast.

Biber was much longer in Salzburg than was Muffat,
and rose to a higher position, being in 1684 created
Kapellmeister.    He was an excellent violinist, and published engraved violin sonatas from Salzburg itself in
two sets, one in 1676 and the other in 1681.    A third
engraved publication was a set of Vespers in 1693 :
all Kapellmeisters were expected to produce some
ecclesiastical music.    He also wrote music for the University plays in Latin.    As for Opera, he looked to Vienna,

though *Arminius* at least received its first performance in Salzburg in 1687 [S 24].

Much influenced by Italian music, Biber's style of composition agreed very well with that of Muffat : antagonism between them was due solely to proper rivalry, a rivalry which was dissolved when Muffat became Kapellmeister of Passau. Biber remained on in Salzburg to rise to the highest influence, an influence which no non-Italian was ever to exercise after his death. Born on the Bohemian border, his Kapellmeistership, his Court position of High Steward and his " von " were to dazzle Leopold Mozart, and to quicken his ambition to do likewise.

It was the Emperor Leopold I who gave Biber his title to the minor nobility : like " von " Dittersdorf, similarly placed with a Kapellmeistership and a Court post, Biber felt a " von " of importance. It is not known how he obtained it, but Dittersdorf tells us how, some half-century or more later, he purchased his through a Viennese agent specialising in titles for 1,100 gulden (nominally £110 or $308, in modern currency probably ten times that amount), and that was at half price !

During the reign of Archbishop Harrach (1709–1727), Salzburg was for a period visited by Antonio Caldara [S 24]. This important Venetian composer exerted as considerable an influence upon Salzburg music as did the residents Biber and Muffat. Religious music was the most important, and this genre was divided into operatic solos and polyphonic choruses. Caldara emphasised this division, the operatic solos typical of the " galant " style of writing, and the choruses of the " learned " art, and introduced mannerisms which lingered. For instance, as Cecil Gray [G 7] has pointed out, when writing in a

minor key, Caldara likes a progression from a flattened
sixth to the augmented fourth, and this survives as late
as Mozart's " learned " Fugue in C minor for two pianos,
K 426. Caldara's religious music, " sublime " Hawkins
calls it, was a challenge taken up by the art of Mozart,
who struggled to sublimate the opposing " galant "
and " learned " into a new and personal style. No
sooner had he achieved this, than Salzburg became
unbearable, and he left his native city for Vienna.

In J. E. Eberlin we meet a composer of considerable
talent who exercised his influence for years to come and
on both the Mozarts. He came to Salzburg at the age of
22 and by 1736, when he was 34, he had grad-
uated to junior positions in both spheres in
which Biber had been so successful. On the purely
Court side he was " Touchesse " or Carver to the Archbishop : on the musical, he was organist. Later, he
became Kapellmeister, and was the holder of this office
when Wolfgang Mozart was born. Francesco Giuseppe
Lolli, who came to Salzburg when Eberlin did, succeeded
him as Kapellmeister. Biber had a son, Karl Heinrich von
Biber, but he rose no higher than Vice-Kapellmeister,
the same rank as Leopold Mozart rose to.

Eight sorts of music can now be listed as practised in
Salzburg at the time Leopold Mozart entered the city
as a University student [S 24].

There would be the ecclesiastical music at the Cathedral : a Mass, treated with no great expenditure of time,
with its learned counterpoint in the choir contrasted
with its flimsy solo work, for which operatic arias were
the model. Organ, orchestra, choir and soloists were all
housed in the west gallery, the music coming dramati-
cally and unseen from behind the worshippers.

St. Peter's ancient foundation was more severe than the Cathedral in its music, and clung longer to the learned style. This was the church in which Michael Haydn became organist, and in which his memorial was to be placed. It is a mere accident, but an interesting point, that one of the monks bore the Haydn surname, R. P. Thaddeus Haydn ; he died in 1767 [S 18]. He had been born in 1703 in Upper Austria, and was clearly no relation of the brothers Joseph and Michael. As Michael Haydn came to Salzburg in 1762, there were two Haydns in Salzburg for five years.

This is music of three sorts, ranging from severely religious at St. Peter's, through choruses at the Cathedral, to solo arias in the same place of operatic ornamentation and texture.

Fourthly, there was purely secular instrumental music. This was essentially social, music for use, Gebrauchsmusik, in fact. Its job was to grace birthdays and weddings, and its chief duty to be fluent and melodious, repeating itself and not cutting things too short. This easy tradition very much suited the torrent of charming ideas which Wolfgang Mozart wished to put on paper when in the mood, writing serenades for the street or the garden, divertimenti for outdoor or indoor celebrations for friends and patrons.

Less important musically and even more grimly Gebrauchsmusik was to herald in, by wind fanfares, succeeding courses or toasts at dinner.

As for secular singing, opera was provided by visiting troupes, and of solo singing within doors of a lieder kind there was little. We have Mozart's K 53, and this makes up our eight sorts of Salzburg music, but the melodies of the people were no more in demand than

were musical settings of favourite poems. Salzburg
music existed as part of ecclesiastical routine and partly
to please Salzburg citizens. In church musical needs
were partly Catholic and partly what the Archbishop
needed to get him through the Sacrament. Of course, the
Catholic need predominated, even Mozart's Archbishop,
Colloredo, who liked things short and tasty, could not
prevent the whole Gloria and the whole Credo being sung.

The secular needs of the wealthy were hearty rather
than fastidious. Just as they demanded good food and
good wine, admired Archbishops who gave them fine
buildings, disliked Archbishops who taxed them too hard
to pay for the same, so they liked good music, plenty of
it, not requiring too much in the way of concentration,
but of obviously good quality, with melody and refine-
ment. They also liked family gambling games, flirtations
and coarse family jokes. It was not a spiritual society, it
would not have nurtured a Romantic : in public, formal
sociability, and in private, unbuttoned family life, rather
excluded any development of Wolfgang Mozart's genius
towards the string quartet or lieder, while giving his
mere talent ample opportunity for a starchy Mass or an
endless Rondo.

It is part of the purpose of this book to mention
happenings outside Salzburg, even for the very reason
that they did not influence the Principality : it shows how
amazingly fortunate Salzburg was in her geographical
position and in the personal abilities of her Archbishops.
In the years 1737–8, when Leopold Mozart was peacefully
studying at the University, the mobs in Vienna were out
in the streets, angrily demonstrating their wounded
patriotism at the continued defeats of the Imperial
armies under Maria Theresa's husband.

Salzburg had not been invaded since the sixteenth century, when the Bavarians made an unopposed entry to dismiss Wolf Dietrich. The Peasants' Revolt and the Counter Reformation had touched her more lightly than most other Germanic lands, and though Jews, as well as Protestants, were from time to time not popular, there was never a St. Bartholomew to disgrace the pages of Salzburg's history.

This history is not only of interest in itself, but is of value in showing the origin of traditions and of ecclesiastical powers which were to affect the Mozarts. Independent Salzburg grew out of Bavaria, and it was into Bavaria that Salzburg lapsed when, a millennium later, Colloredo, Mozart's Archbishop, fled to Vienna during the Napoleonic wars. There is thus a certain neatness about Salzburg's history.

The Dukes of Bavaria, however, did not themselves appoint the early ecclesiastics, who were never Bavarians. Thus the first of all, St. Rupert, who built a monastery on the rock of Salzburg was a Frenchman, as we would now call him, and as he would not have called himself. He visited a Duke of Bavaria for one of the many Diets at Worms. When the district was civilised enough to demand a Bishop, it was an Irish priest, Virgil, who travelled from France to the reigning Duke and thence to the monastery of St. Peter on the rock of Salzburg. He needed home and food and subordinates and he was appointed to the conveniently vacant Abbacy. Even after the first Cathedral of Salzburg was built and became the Metropolitan Cathedral Church of the Province, the Archbishops of Salzburg continued to be pluralist Abbots of St. Peter until 1023, when a new Archbishop was consecrated who did not possess this plurality. An

independent Abbot was a factor in the first performance
of Mozart's Mass in C minor, K 427 at a time when he
feared arrest by the Archbishop, for though nominally
subordinate to the Archbishops, the Abbots had considerable influence and power.

Between 1041 and 1060 there was a period of renewed
plurality which did not recur.

Juvavum (the old Roman name was still used) grew,
the influence of Bavaria receded. Right to mint its own
money was granted to " Salzburg " when Otto III was
Emperor in Vienna, Imperial–Papal relations being
unusually cordial. The Archbishops became Cardinals
almost as a matter of course, the first to wear the red hat
being the 18th Archbishop, consecrated in 1088. All the
Archbishops important to us in this study of Mozart
became Cardinals and Papal Legates as well. Lastly, in
1278, the final touch was given to the Archdiocese when
its Head was created a Prince of the Empire by Rudolph
of Hapsburg. For over five hundred years thereafter
the Prince Archbishops of Salzburg, in unbroken line,
ruled over a large Principality with an authority both
spiritual and temporal. This authority increased rather
than diminished, their subjects were kept in increasing
subordination, and Pope and Emperor could be played
off against each other with refreshing effect.

When the Pope was in the ascendant, as for instance
during part of the pontificate of Gregory VII, the Archbishop would in fact be chosen by the local nobility who
exerted their influence through and on the Cathedral
Chapter who nominally made the appointment. When the
Emperor was the more powerful, the appointment was
conveyed as a wish to the Cathedral Chapter, a wish
they dared not ignore. But no Prince-Archbishop, once

appointed, ever carried his gratitude to Emperor or to Pope to the length of martyrdom. If " his side " weakened, he would cautiously move over to the other. If we say the Archbishops of Salzburg were like the Vicars of Bray, this is true provided that we remember that they were all unquestionably Catholics, the Bray variations being between the two extremes of Hildebrandism, by which the Pope was an invisible Prince-Archbishop alongside them, or of secularism, by which they were primarily Princes of the Empire and their relationship with the Pope purely spiritual and ecclesiastical. In this secular theory, the Emperor became the second, invisible, administrator. No Archbishop could rule quite alone, and in the short and infrequent spells of Imperial–Papal harmony, there were three rulers in Salzburg, one visible and two invisible. Though this arrangement might have seemed secure and peaceful enough, some of Salzburg's rulers, such as Archbishop Gebhard, occupied the cliff tops and started those fortifications which now loom over us as we discuss our cakes and ale on the tables of the garden restaurants below.

What had been started against the possibility of Imperial or Transalpine anger came in very useful when defying the tumults of their own subjects.

During a period of unusually bitter Imperial–Papal strife, the Emperor (Barbarossa) vigorously installed a protégé of his, Adalbert, as Archbishop. Adalbert's uncle was Leopold, Duke of Austria, who captured Richard Coeur de Lion when this King of England was returning from a Crusade, as a result of which capture an irate Pope, a zealous Crusader himself, excommunicated the Duke of Austria. His nephew the Archbishop of Salzburg following the by then established policy of the balance of power, of neutrality and of diplomacy, acted as mediator. His uncle became very ill : his illness was the cue for the Archbishop. Hopes for bliss in the next world induced the Duke to return the ransom money to the English Court (Richard had been of course immediately ransomed) and in return the Archbishop gave his uncle Holy Communion and promised to have him buried in a churchyard G9.

Another Archbishop who played the part of mediator was Eberhard. To put the matter shortly, this was in a war, with tiny armies of under a thousand, between the Tyrol and Bavaria. The Archbishop was able to obtain a year's truce, and to prolong this truce, after tempers had cooled, for a second year, and so to eventual peace.

But to their own subjects, the Prince-Archbishops could be harsher. Leonhard II expelled the Jews in 1498 and soon after took to himself many of the rights hitherto enjoyed by the citizens. As we gaze at the fortress of Hohen-Salzburg on the top of its mountain, we may imagine this Prince-Archbishop taking refuge there from his townsfolk in 1511 with greater success than the Archbishop of Canterbury in the Tower of London in 1381.

While Leonhard II's acts of oppression were creating that hatred which culminated in the peasants' risings of 1525, in the greater Empire beyond the borders of Salzburg the first stirrings of the Renaissance were felt in the reign of the Hapsburg monarch, Maximilian I. It was he who so firmly established his family on the Imperial Throne that after him his successors were always elected to the throne of the Holy Roman Empire. And at the same time they ruled by personal right and hereditary descent those large tracts of lands which might

loosely be termed, in the language of to-day, " Austria."
Learning revived, science progressed, and a legal system
based upon what was considered to be that of ancient
Rome was practised. In 1517 Luther began his reformation, but this movement was not felt in Salzburg for a
surprisingly long while, though at last even Salzburg
became a place where there were persecutors and persecuted.

Peasants' revolts, too, were less severe in Salzburg than
elsewhere in the Empire. Tension between the Duke of
Bavaria and the Archbishop of Salzburg at one time gave
the peasants hope of success, but the Archbishop,
Leonhard, crushed it with some ease after a revolt which
did not last more than a year, and was more lenient to
his captives and to his subjects than most other rulers.
By 1587, when Wolf Dietrich became Archbishop at the
early age of 28, Salzburg was about to begin its period
of splendour.

This young man was a grandson of a Medici and had
the outlook and instincts of an Italian of his times. The
most picturesque of his actions was his building the
Mirabell Palace for his mistress, Salome Alt, in 1607. In
this woman and in their many children, Wolf Dietrich
found a genuine family life natural to him and from which
his profession debarred him. It was far removed from
mere licentiousness.

His relations with the Pope were cool, cooler even
than those of the average Archbishop of Salzburg, and
although one might suppose Salome Alt to be the cause,
it appears that it was Salzburg's tolerance of Protestants
within her frontiers which was the real trouble. Wolf
Dietrich was a genuine Catholic, and his relationship
with Salome Alt does not appear to have led him to

question the wisdom of the celibacy of the clergy, but, after all, even Protestants were his subjects and he did not want any outsider, even the Pope, to bully them.

Such bullying was reserved for himself and was restricted to levying severe taxes on his whole Province, to pay for his stables, the Marstall, now the site of the Festival Theatre, the upkeep of the Mirabell, and to pay for religious building, too. There was the monastery on the Kapuzinerberg, for instance, the churches of St. Francis and St. Sebastian, and, above all, a new Cathedral. The old one had been burnt in 1508, and was to be rebuilt in the great, splendid modern style to plans by Sanatino Solaris, and opposite this Palace of God could be the Palace of the Archbishop, the Residenz, as was only appropriate.

Thus worn by taxation, the people of Salzburg, though they appear not to have disliked Wolf Dietrich, were inactive when Bavarian troops invaded the Principality. It was an opportune moment for a Duke of Bavaria to claim again lordship over Salzburg, for the Pope at the time happened not to be a Medici, and the Emperor, Rudolf II, was closing his long and dismal reign. The old game of playing one off against the other or of receiving help from both if menaced by neither was for the time at an end.

Wolf Dietrich had to leave his Principality and his Province, and he attempted to escort Salome Alt to Italy. They were stopped and separated. Salome Alt was allowed to continue into exile, and the Archbishop was imprisoned for the last five years of his life in the Festung built by his predecessors above his Metropolitan City.

Though neither Pope nor Emperor would help Wolf

Dietrich, this did not mean that either intended that Bavaria should dominate Salzburg. The Duke withdrew, and the new Archbishop, Markus Sitticus, continued with the Cathedral whose foundations had been laid by Wolf Dietrich. When he in turn died, the building proceeded under the next, no other than the great Paris Lodron, after whom one of the main streets of the city is named. He was a member of a powerful family, whose descendants were very much alive in Salzburg down to Mozart's day. Lodron firmly gathered up the reins which Wolf Dietrich had let drop, and kept quite clear from the confused religious wars, which French ambitions often fomented, not always simply just of Catholic versus Protestant. Salzburg Principality was nevertheless and unquestionably and necessarily always most orthodox in its Catholicism, yet Lodron never permitted Protestants to be persecuted, and always allowed them that measure of religious freedom which in fact is almost all that they actually take, even to-day : Sunday morning meetings in each other's farms to sing hymns, nowadays to an harmonium.

It is often claimed that the main route from Germany to Italy lies through Salzburg, and that is why the city shows so much mingling of Italian and German culture. But (the question of the mingling culture apart for the moment) such is the opposite of the truth. It is more important to realise that no main routes to anywhere went through Salzburg. Even to-day the Orient Express keeps south on its way from Switzerland to Vienna. Owing to Salzburg's unimportance as a route centre, Lodron was able to keep his Principality at peace and practise tolerance within those limits which family pride and a proper respect for the truth as he saw it, admitted. Salzburg,

almost alone of all the units which went to make up the
Holy Roman Empire, did not become a pawn in Power
Politics, while to the north of Salzburg thousands of
square miles were laid waste.

This is perhaps all the more remarkable as the boundaries of the temporal Principality were not exactly those
of the spiritual Province [53].   In parts which were
indubitably in the Tyrol or in Styria lived clergy owing
spiritual obedience to him, and a whole Diocese, that of
Chiemsee, made a pocket in Bavaria all by itself.  It is
true that at one time the temporal boundaries of the
Principality stretched as far as the Inn, but the Archbishops never minded retreating in a spirit of Christian
humility provided it was not very far, and Chiemsee was
left all by itself because of the Duke of Bavaria pushing
his frontier out at the expense of the Archbishops,
who displayed their energy in architecture not in land
grabbing like Bavaria or still more the Hapsburg family,
who swallowed Styria, Carinthia and Upper Austria, so
that the lands under direct Imperial authority reached
to the Archbishops' boundaries.  But even the Imperial
Hapsburg appetite stopped in time to leave Archbishop
Lodron in peace to build the University as well as new
defences on the heights of the Monchsberg and the
Kapuzinerberg: he had presumably not forgotten the
fate of Archbishop Wolf Dietrich.

The Thun family now rises into prominence.  They
provided the Archbishop after Lodron, and there is a
print of this priest on his triumphal return from receiving
his hat.

Marlborough's Blenheim campaign occurred during
the reign of another member of the Thun family, he who
gave new bells to Wolf Dietrich's Glockenspiel from

money which he had made in the Austrian East India
Company. Thun managed as well as Paris Lodron in the
task of keeping his Principality out of war. The Allies
marched no further south and east than Augsburg, in
which town there happened to be a bookbinder in business whose name was J. G. Mozart, one of a line of
bookbinders.

We are indeed nearing the Mozartian era : between
this Thun and the first of the Mozartian Archbishops,
Firmian, is only Franz Anton Graf von Harrach, 1709–27,
to whom the usual splendid folio of praise was dedicated
and whose chief task in life was to remodel the Mirabell
Palace.

The Archbishops who influenced the lives of the
Mozarts are several : Colloredo was the last and most
important : Schrattenbach, Colloredo's predecessor, was
the second most important, and thirdly, the earliest was
Archbishop Leopold von Firmian. Between Firmian and
Schrattenbach occur minor figures of short duration.

Salzburg Catholicism had become less tolerant since
the happy days of Lodron, and Firmian prepared to
banish the Protestants. He issued an edict :—

" We Leopold, by the Grace of God, Archbishop
of Salzburg, Legate of the Holy See Apostolical,
and Primate of Germany etc.,[1] To all our Vice
Deans, Bailiffs, Provosts, Governors, their Substi-
tutes, Judges, and to all our Officers and Subjects,
Greeting."

Then the Decree follows. Its first portion shows what
grounds there are for action basing itself on " the natural

[1] Our translation is from the contemporary *Account of the Sufferings*, printed in
London in 1732 : A 10 and A 11 in the Bibliography.

Laws and Constitutions of the Empire," because the matter of religious toleration was one which concerned the Emperor, at least nominally. Then, more particularly, " the Fidelity which was due to us as their Lord and Prince " was not given, the Decree complains. The Protestants indeed failed to " pay all the Obedience and Respect due to the Spiritual and Temporal Regencies." They (the Protestants) had been given freedom : " Every one of these might exercise his Religion in secret in his own House (agreeably to the Constitution of the Empire) . . . but for disturbing the publick Tranquillity (they) endeavoured to kindle the Flames of a Religious War throughout the Roman Empire. As our Honour, our Dignity, and our Authority, in the Quality of an Archbishop and Sovereign Prince . . ." was involved, the Protestants would be banished, but on a strictly undemocratic basis. The landless man must leave at once, the landed gentry may have time to sell his estates first.

The Protestants were given a passport : " Whereas the Bearer of this, who professeth the Protestant Religion, Langprandtner by Name, Servant at Hayd, in the County of Gastein, is obliged to go out of the Archiepiscopal Dominions, and leave the Country, the Magistrate is ready to assist him for that Purpose, and give him a well-attested Certificate of his Birth, Pedigree, and Apology . . . he is obliged upon the Account of having forsaken the Roman Catholic Religion, which alone is exercised and suffered in these Archiepiscopal Dominions, to go out of them . . ."

These documents clearly show the dual power of the Archbishop, that he drew his temporal power from being a Prince of the Roman Empire, and that, while he wished his Protestants to go away, he intended no massacre of St. Bartholomew.

Goethe treated of an incident in this Protestant exodus from Salzburg in *Hermann and Dorothea*, though placing the scene nominally later.

Perhaps the comparative mildness of the exodus of no less than 30,000 Protestants from the Province of Salzburg in 1731 and 1732 was due in some part to the ameliorative influence exercised by Frederick William of Prussia.

With the arrival of the young Leopold Mozart into Salzburg from Augsburg to study at the University in 1736, only four years after the departure of the Protestants, we enter into the Mozartian era.

The struggle of ambition against lack of money caused Leopold Mozart to form a habit of duplicity. Later in life this habit became stultifying to its possessor, and possibly a cause of mirth to others. But the occasion of the birth of this habit very nearly brought Leopold to disaster. Sent to Salzburg by the Benedictines to study theology, he in fact studied law : one assumes he hoped his patrons would not learn of this, but they did so, and cut off his only source of revenue. He thus had to enter domestic service, and became a valet de chambre to an Arch Canon and President of the Salzburg Chapter : there was no equivalent to the English " Dean " nearer than this.

A valet de chambre ranked high : much higher, for instance, than unlettered servants like lackeys or footmen. His son Wolfgang was to be ranked with the Arch-bishop's valets, on the same social plane as Wolfgang has it. We are so far away from this sort of society that we find it most difficult to accept the fact that an educated

c

University student could support himself by accepting
work as an upper servant.

Johann Baptise Count Thurn Valsassine and Taxis
seems to have been a kind and broad-minded patron.
His valet de chambre was encouraged to study the violin
and he accepted the dedication of a volume of three-part
sonatas written by Leopold in 1740. This little effort
passed hardly noticed, the big musical event of the year
in Salzburg being a performance of Bernasconi's *Temi-*
*stocle* to a libretto by Metastasio.

The Emperor, Charles VI not utterly troubled by the
advances of the Turks and the retreats of his son-in-law,
who had indeed returned to Vienna, composed an opera
which he himself conducted at the harpsichord, con-
trolling his nobility singing away on the stage of the
palace theatre. When October came round, the Emperor
went hunting as usual, and heated and hungry, dined off
mushrooms stewed in oil. He was seized with violent
pains : gout, perhaps, or colic. He died, while the
Empress and his son-in-law were dissolved in tears. His
daughter, Maria Theresa, pregnant, was away.

So while Leopold Mozart was writing *Christ Buried*
for Lent, the unprotected Empire was the object of
European greed. Frederick the Great invaded Silesia.
The Duke of Bavaria declared himself Archduke of
Austria. It was this second act which might have
involved Salzburg, not the greater menace of Prussia.

By his claim, the Elector of Bavaria (who was secretly
backed by the French in an effort to reduce the power of
the Hapsburgs) in effect claimed all those territories which
were ruled by the Emperor in his personal capacity as a
Hapsburg, and which Charles VI, as Duke of Austria,
had on his deathbed wished to bequeath to his daughter,

Maria Theresa. But Maria Theresa claimed all the lands and powers which would have been hers had she been a man, that is, the Imperial title, the nominal sway of the Empire, the Kingdom of Hungary and the personal rule as landlord of what we might loosely name " Austria." Maria Theresa, ruling alone, was so far from trembling at the pretensions of the Elector of Bavaria, that she talked of tidying her frontier herself, and at his expense. This untidy salient lay to the north of Salzburg, and it is typical of the history of the Principality that the Archbishop was not drawn into this War of the Austrian Succession, nor did Bavarian, British, French or Imperial troops march across his territory.

One friend, though a secret one, helped Maria Theresa, and that was the King of England. In his capacity of George II he paid her a secret subsidy, but in his capacity of Elector of Hanover he was induced by Louis XV to observe a strict neutrality. George II's Cabinet approved of the subsidy as tending towards the preservation of the balance of power which was already, so it seemed, tilting dangerously in France's favour. She had already invaded Bohemia in support of Bavaria and succeeded in having her puppet the Elector crowned King of Bohemia and, later, even crowned Emperor under the style of Charles VII, at Frankfort on 12th February 1742. Added to these troubles, Maria Theresa had to defend herself against a renewed attack by Frederick of Prussia, who had already taken all he wanted, but whose nature, as he himself admitted, was to make war.

Somewhat fortified by the loyalty of her Hungarian nobles and by English Cabinet changes under Carteret, Maria Theresa rearranged her advisers. The intriguing Bartenstein became Chancellor, and he in turn promoted

Count Uhfeld. Meanwhile Rudolf Joseph, of the House of Colloredo-Mansfeld, whose eldest son, Hieronymus, was to become the last Prince-Archbishop of Salzburg, only retained his position in the Court by bowing to the loathed Bartenstein, a degree of suppleness which in time made him Imperial Vice-Chancellor and Conference Minister.

Maria Theresa's army invested Linz and crossed the Inn to the north of Salzburg, while the Tyrolese aided her by invading Bavaria from their side. Munich fell the very day the false Emperor was crowned in Frankfort. This landless monarch offered thereupon to renounce his pretension. He died not long afterwards, though still known as Charles VII. His successor as Elector of Bavaria, however, made it clear that there were no claims at all on the Imperial title, a declaration for which Maria Theresa was the less grateful as she had bought off Prussia by ceding the southern part of Silesia and had George II's guarantee of subsequent Peace. She had retaken Bohemia from the French and Bavarian invaders.

Archbishop Firmian died in 1744, friendly enough with Maria Theresa for a younger brother of his to be appointed by her Governor of Lombardy, but not so friendly as to incur hostilities with France or the baffled resentment of the Elector of Bavaria. Count Leichtenstein was the next Archbishop ; his reign was short and did not affect that junior member of the Archiepiscopal orchestra Leopold Mozart, who had, in fact, while fighting was going on all round Salzburg, or so it must have seemed, made definite advances in his career. The University had played his music to a Latin play, and he had secured the appointment of violin teacher to the Cathedral singing

boys who were taught in the Choir School founded by
Wolf Dietrich. Lastly, he was appointed one of the Court
composers, of which there were several; Leopold's
position was very junior in comparison with that of
Eberlin himself. These were his worldly circumstances
when he met his future wife.

St. Gilgen is to-day a beautiful town on the shores of
Lake Wolfgang, reached after travelling a mountain road
from Salzburg which rises high over the watershed at
Hof, and then descends to the shores of Lake Fuschl with
its Schloss, and so through another pass to St. Gilgen.
In a long white house at the other end of the town and by
the shores of Lake Wolfgang lived Anna Maria Bertel
or Pertel. She was a young woman of twenty-three or
so, and lived with her widowed mother, Eva Rosina,
born Ultmann. Her father, Wolfgang Nikolous Pertel
had been a local landowner, and in the family Schloss,
Huttenstein, Anna Maria had been born. W. N. Pertel,
apparently a younger son, secured the appointment of
Warden of a charity and took up his residence in the
white house in the town until his death.

We know very little about the wooing of Anna Maria
Pertel and Leopold Mozart. We do know from a reference
of Leopold's that they were in love for some years before
they could marry, and we may assume they met in Salzburg, for it was obviously more likely that Anna Maria
would sometimes visit the capital than that the personal
servant of the " Dean " of Salzburg would have time to
visit the shores of Lake Wolfgang. During their courtship Leopold found independent work in the orchestra
among the violins and wrote some Church music.

To-day, Anna Maria's relationship with both her native
town and her son Wolfgang is commemorated by a

delightful fountain in the main square, in which a small
boy ravishes nightingales by his violin playing.

After some years of courtship the couple were married
in the suburban church of Aigen on 21st November
1747. " The handsomest couple in Salzburg," as they
were called, took up residence in a flat on the third floor
of what became Getreidegasse 9, which is now the upper
of the two floors occupied by the Mozart Museum. The
house, then as now, looks into a small court, or short
street. In 1747 this area was larger and was named the
Löchelplatz, but it was so badly illuminated at night
that Leopold Mozart could not easily find the keyhole of
the outer door [M 20]. Beyond this courtyard was the
turbulent whitish river, the Salzach, shallow, broad and
fast. The owner of Getreidegasse 9 was a Herr Hagenauer
who became very friendly with his tenants the Mozarts.
At the back of the house was the rear portion of the row
facing the University Church, so there was no outlook
on this side, and no garden to No. 9. It is sometimes
stated that the University and Church could be seen from
the windows by the Mozarts : there is one narrow slit
through which a glimpse of open space can be obtained,
but that is all.

The couple started under good auspices. The husband
was unusually intelligent and hard-working, a good user
of money, and thrifty. His wife was good and loyal,
a strict Catholic, like her husband.

For a while after his marriage Leopold Mozart's
worldly circumstances did not much change. The death
of Archbishop Leichtenstein and the succession of
Dietrichstein made no difference to him [S 13], and Eberlin
continued at the head of the Court music. Lotter
of Augsburg engraved *IX Toccate e fughe per l'organo* for

Eberlin, and the composer himself conducted from the organ his *Componimeto sacro* :  Leopold Mozart, not yet Vice-Kapellmeister, was quite obscured.

In the dark, low-ceilinged, but large-roomed Löchelplatz flat, grim Nature was at her task of eighteenth-century birth control.  A boy was born nine months after the marriage and christened Johann Joachim, but he died in 1749.  On 18th June 1749, a girl was born and christened after her mother and paternal grandmother.  She, too, died.  It was not until 30th July 1751 that a baby destined to live appeared.  She, like her dead sister, was christened Maria Anne, and has become immortal as Nannerl :  more correctly, Nannrl, the roll of the rl being something hardly possible for an English tongue.

In the same year as Nannerl's birth, there came into Salzburg a young musician of 23, Anton Cajetan Adlgasser, " von der Insel in Bayerne " [D1].  He had been a pupil of Eberlin and had been educated in Italy at Archiepiscopal expense, and now, his education in Italian taste completed, he took up his appointment of Cathedral organist and Court cembalist.

On 4th November 1752 a son was born to the Mozarts and named Johann Karl :  this poor little baby died next year.  As no child was born in 1753, the household consisted of mother, father, the dying Karl and the thriving Nannerl.  However, in Salzburg this was a most important year, " for the glory of a new light was risen in the heavens over Salzburg, and the most reverend and exalted prince, S.R.I. Lord of Lords SIGISMUNDUS CHRISTOPHORUS of the most ancient lineage of those most illustrious S.R.I. Counts of SCHRATTENBACH has come to the guidance of the Archbishopric of

Salzburg " ^A 8^, the unimportant reigning Archbishop of
a few years having died.

Schrattenbach, last Prince-Archbishop but one, and
second only to Colloredo in influence on the lives of the
Mozarts, came, as the poet of *Splendor lucis novae in coelo*
very truly says, of an exalted family, as indeed did all the
Archbishops except the sixteenth-century Leonhard von
Keutschach. Schrattenbach had a brother, Count Franz
Anton von Schrattenbach of Brunn, whom the Mozarts
visited in 1767. As for the Colloredos, we have already
met one in the Cabinet of the Empress : another we may
now introduce, Graf Karl, Minister to the Court of St.
James. His nephew, Hieronymus and the Archbishop
to be, was just of age.[1]

The principal characters in the Mozartian drama are
crowding on the stage now that Schrattenbach is there.
Franz Ignaz Lipp came from Eggenfelden in Bavaria,
and he was appointed second Cathedral organist, second
to Adlgasser : he was a useful rather than a polished
musician, he had a good tenor voice and could manage
the violin, but was mocked at by the Mozarts. At the
time of his arrival his little daughter, Maria Magdalena,
was four or five : later on she was the cause of Lipp-
Mozartian wrangling, especially when she married
Michael Haydn and became a singer at the Archbishop's
Court.

Johann Andreas Schachtner also came from Bavaria,
and could play both violin and 'cello. His main position,
however, was that of Court Trumpeter : he was a man of
more culture than most Salzburg musicians and therefore

---

[1] Acknowledgments to sources of information from books are given by a code
reference to the bibliography, but for this and other references to the Colloredo
family special thanks must be given to H.E. the Austrian Minister.

(and this can be written without a trace of irony) became
a friend of Leopold Mozart. He was later to translate the
Italian text of *Idomeneo* into German, and he wrote the
libretto of *Zaide*. Other friends which the couple in the
modest Löchelplatz flat made about this time included
the Abbé Bullinger, the tame cleric of the Chief Chamberlain's household, the Arco family. The Abbé became
tutor to one of the Arco sons, Leopold, who was taught
the violin by Leopold Mozart himself. This friendliness
with an ecclesiastic means the more as the Abbé was the
man Wolfgang chose to break to his father the dreadful
news of the death of Frau Mozart in Paris. The Abbé
was a trusted friend, a good man. The family life of the
Mozarts was as spotless as their Catholicism was above
reproach.

In 1755, the year before Wolfgang's birth, his father
was working on the MS. of a textbook on how to play
the violin, and was already in communication with the
printer of Augsburg, named Lotter, who had engraved
for Eberlin. However, he was not at this date busy sending prose, but music. In a letter of 6th November he
sent the MS. score of a composition named *The Peasant's
Wedding*. In this sort of music Leopold excelled, and
showed himself as a humorist, if a somewhat simple one.
A later chapter will discuss Leopold's influence as a
composer on his son : we might now just allude to music
such as his *Sleigh Ride*, *Hunt* and *Divertimento Militaire*,
and other works in which simple effects were executed
by barrel organs, pistol shots, ordinary lip whistling,
bagpipes, bells, side drums and other unusual additions
to the orchestra. Leopold was never fertile in ideas in
the strictly musical sense of the word " idea," but he had
a fund of low inventiveness which would have suited

Schikaneder very well had that impresario come along
in 1755 with the text of *The Magic Flute* in one hand and
a commission in the other.

Not that Leopold Mozart's devotion to the art of
music can be in question. J. S. Bach had bagpipes in
*The Peasant Cantata*, Wolfgang had his " Turkish "
music, Haydn his high spirits, Beethoven his rural band
in the *Pastoral*, and Couperin many effective jokes for
the clavecin. But in the case of Leopold Mozart the
inclination towards mere fun and frolic was strong, and
it is a side of his character which could not be deduced
from his notions on money, social position or the importance of intrigue, which make him like a serious accountant, honest but a little crafty, and very good at managing
board meetings. That this serious accountant of our
imagination should also write circus music, have a real
love of and discernment for good music as well, and on
top of that enjoy the most appalling and coarse family
jokes merely shows how complicated we all are.

Meanwhile, in Vienna, intrigue was beginning on a
grand scale. Angered by the haughty tone of Whitehall
and thinking George II perfidious in countenancing the
transfer of Silesia from the Hapsburg dominions to
Prussia, Maria Theresa started a flattering correspondence
with the Pompadour. As for the indignity of writing to
a whore—" have I not flattered Farinelli ? "[1].[C2]. This
letter-writing was kept secret, even the Emperor Francis
was not informed.

A son was born to the Mozarts at their flat at eight
o'clock in the evening of 27th January 1756. The

[1] Farinelli, famous castrato male singer who became very influential at the
Spanish Court.

next morning at ten the new baby was baptized in the Cathedral by the Town Chaplain, Leopold Lamprecht. From the Cathedral Register itself it may be noted that this new baby was the only baptism that day : Lamprecht was not, indeed, kept very busy. He had had to baptize only seven, including the Mozart baby, between 18th January and 4th February.

Johann Theophilus Pergmayer, a town councillor and a merchant, acted as godfather and gave one of his names, Theophilus, to the new baby : it seems rather sad that this good man faded out of the baby's life. He is not included in the long strings of names with which the Mozart family letters were to be so often prolonged.

Joannes was given him by his father, whose name it also was.

His maternal grandfather was a Wolfgang, and so comes not only the Christian name by which Mozart is usually best known, but the one most prized by his parents. The Feast of St. Wolfgang was on 31st October, and this date, following the usual custom, became Wolfgang's name day, duly celebrated from year to year by all his friends until the end. Indeed, name days took precedence over birthdays, which are rarely mentioned in correspondence.

Chrysostum, a name not to be found among the infant's immediate forebears was the last name chosen. But we remember that most beautiful prayer composed by Chrysostum, Archbishop of Constantinople, "Almighty God, who has given us grace at this time of one accord to make our common supplications unto thee . . ." and may think it a happy inspiration that the great musical poet just born should be named after the great Greek poet of the liturgy.

Theophilus, of course, means Lover of God, and Amadeus means the same thing, in Latin instead of Greek. Thus, in all its grandeur,

Joannes Chrysostomus Wolfgangus Theophilus,

or, more simply,

Wolfgang Amadeus.

# The First Salzburg Period

## THE INFANT

*Residence :*      Flat in the Löchelplatz
*Archbishop :*    Schrattenbach

THIS PERIOD STRETCHES from Wolfgang's birth until he was taken to Munich by his father on 12th January 1762. During the whole of this period the Seven Years War excited Europe, without involving Salzburg. No troops crossed, much less, invaded, the Principality, and indeed Schrattenbach had less difficulty in maintaining the traditional neutrality than did Paris Lodron or Firmian in their days. Maria Theresa was bold enough to create a league against Prussia, whom she had never forgiven for the theft of Silesia. Those who see her portrait in The Queen of the Night can point to the insatiable enmity which the theft of her daughter by Sarastro caused her to feel ; in some other respects the parallel breaks down. Pompadour was encouraging, and was used by the French Court to allow Maria Theresa to suppose that France was a friend, though in reality neither Maria Theresa nor any other Hapsburg was to be allowed to aggrandise herself too much. This French policy was of great hidden influence on the fate of Salzburg. A Hapsburg, completely victorious over Prussia and with France as a firm ally, with eastern borders securely protected against both Russia and Turkey, might well have deemed the Imperial title to be more than merely nominal. Prince-Archbishops everywhere, as well as Grand Dukes and even Electors, would then have felt that they had a real as well as a nominal master.

Far less happy than the Archbishop of Salzburg was that King of Saxony and of Poland (a pluralist Monarch) who appointed J. S. Bach as his Saxon Court Composer. He had already once before been forced to leave his capital, Dresden, because of an advancing Prussian army, and was doomed to do this again, and to retire to his Polish capital of Warsaw.

The Archduke Joseph, eldest son of the union of Francis and Maria Theresa, who was later to be Emperor under the style of Joseph II, secured his succession to the Imperial title as we will see on p. 54.

His father's illness in 1763 heralded peace. Maria Theresa began to find her war altogether too exhausting. Her friends cooled, and her family tendered advice. Catherine of Russia, German born, began to be infected by the deep suspicions and lethargy of her subjects. Bavaria became so bored that Leopold Mozart could write home from Munich in 1762 that " they talk of war as little as if there were no war."

There is nothing to show that the Mozarts at home bothered about the war news. When at home, Leopold was busy pushing the Augsburg printer to produce the sheets of his *Violinschule*, and when he heard the cries of the tiny Wolfgang, may merely have wondered whether the new baby would live, or join his two elder brothers in a better world. When at last the book was off machine, it had to be bound by someone, and was not bound in

Salzburg. Lotter was a printer and engraver, not a binder. We remember in this context that Leopold's two younger brothers were both binders in the same small city as Lotter.

Its author is described on the title page as " Hochfurstl. Salzburgischen Cammermusicus," and he gives an introduction, twelve detailed chapters on various aspects of violin technique, and a dedication to Schrattenbach which is charming and, more unusual in eighteenth-century dedications, sensible. Addressing this Prince of the Holy Roman Empire (Schrattenbach was not at this time a Cardinal), Leopold Mozart writes " How many would have had, in the increase of their years, to famish in want and poverty and to be a burden on the community as useless citizens of the world, if your Grace had not graciously provided instruction for such, according to their talent and ability, in this or that branch of knowledge ? " Leopold Mozart goes on to express his confidence that Schrattenbach will extend his protection to the book, as a general patron of the arts and sciences, but especially the art of music.

It is clear from the general tone of Leopold Mozart's Preface that he took the deepest interest in his job of teaching the violin, an activity which took all the time he could spare from his Court duties. He taught the boys of the Choir School, and had as many private pupils as he could fit in.

This Preface is dated 26th July 1756, six months after the birth of Wolfgang, and Leopold Mozart had hoped for publication by the preceding 28th February, when Schrattenbach celebrated his birthday. As when the Preface was written the sheets had obviously not been bound nor indeed the preliminary matter printed, Leopold

could not have been much in advance for the 1757 birthday. The Archbishop's name day was on 25th July, so
that, too, had been missed.

Little care was taken of mothers in those days. There
was no question of Frau Mozart going to hospital, or
away for a holiday.

Leopold casually dismisses her performance : " By
the way, I want to tell you that on the evening of the 27th
of January my wife was delivered of a boy and, indeed,
with success. She was unexpectedly weak when the
after-birth was removed. But now, thank God, both
mother and child are well."

The birth of his book, indeed, cost more. Lotter was
not a publisher in the modern sense, and Leopold secured
300 gulden, about thirty pounds or seventy-eight
dollars, out of his widowed mother's estate in Augsburg.
Frau Mozart of Augsburg had allowed his brothers a like
sum during her life and his guardian, Canon Grabner,
favoured his publishing venture and helped him to secure
the money. The first favourable review appeared in 1757,
Marpurg writing in *Historisch-kritische Beytrage* ᴹ ¹⁰
" One has long desired a work of this kind, but hardly
dared to expect it." In 1766 a Dutch translation appeared
in Harlem. In 1769 Leopold Mozart sold out his first
edition and gave Lotter an order to reprint. Soon after,
a musician in the Household of the Duke of Orleans
translated the work and had it printed in Paris as being by
the " Compositeur et Directeur de la Musique de
Monseigneur l'Archévêque de Saltzbourg " which, of
course, he hardly was, Eberlin occupying that position.

When we look at the flat in the Löchelplatz, large in
area, low in ceiling, and quite without any of the modern
helps to life which we now consider essential, in which

1b  Leopold  Mozart

1a  A Romantic looks out on the Lochelplatz, c. 1820

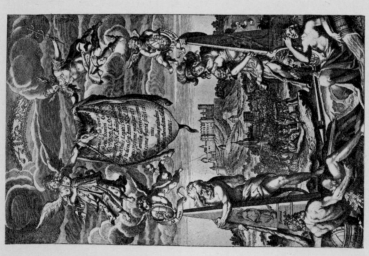

2   The Princely Priests.   Folio illustrations glorifying Thun (left) and Schrattenbach (right)

there was, in 1755-6, a girl aged between four and five, a newly-born baby and a weak mother, it is a wonder how a work of proved scholarly merit could have been written. Wolfgang could write a strong and living symphonic movement during a game of billiards. But geniuses apart, and in the ordinary course of life, the composition by Leopold Mozart of his *Violinschule* in his flat is indeed astonishing.

It was not, of course, as if he had nothing else to do at home. Looking in from time to time would be Schachtner the Court trumpeter : in attendance on Frau Mozart was Dr. Niderl. Wenzel Hebelt would come for a violin lesson, and so would other professionals, so well was he esteemed. Amateur pupils of course would usually be visited in their own palatial and, in our eyes, picturesque homes.

1756 was the year in which Kajetan Biber entered the Archbishop's service, as did three other violinists, Holtzl, Vogt, and Schwartzmann, who also doubled with the bassoon [D1]. The following year a Silesian (Seidle) arrived and then, an Italian among these German names, Caspar Cristelli, a composer and 'cellist from Vienna. Eberlin, the German in position against the pretensions of the Italian, "wrote as much and as rapidly as Telemann " as Marpurg observed in the same publication as that in which he praised the *Violinschule*. There was no opening among deaths or departures to help Leopold : the chief of these was only one of the Court composers, Johann Georg Paris, a man far from being of the Kapellmeister class.

So far we have seen Salzburg as a Court with a petty Sovereign, with landed aristocracy, with professional men, shopkeepers and musicians. In Sigismund Haffner

D

we meet someone of the more modern type, the wealthy
and powerful man of business. He was mainly a banker,
with correspondents who would cash his drafts in various
parts of Europe. He was also a merchant and acted
thirdly in the way we nowadays associate with building
societies : he advanced money for building, taking the
title deeds as security. He and his family have their name
immortalised in two of Wolfgang Mozart's compositions.

There being but one Archbishop and but one Haffner,
the two found it convenient to settle taxation direct. For
the consideration of 26,000 gulden (£2,600 or $7,000)
payable annually, he was able to secure his business
ledgers exempt from examination $^{W1}$. This arrangement continued after his death in 1772, on the petition
of his heir. In a sense this is the French system of the
"fermier général," except that the Haffners could only
operate within their own business, while the great Louis
gave, for yearly annuities, whole Provinces.

To return to Leopold Mozart. He and his household
were strict Catholics, and no visitor to their flat would
be in any doubt of their religious faith. An orphan,
with an ecclesiastic for a guardian, an ecclesiastical
education in a monastery choir, paid for at Salzburg
University by the Benedictines and lastly in the service
of an official with some resemblance to a Cathedral Dean,
Leopold would either have had to rebel or to succumb.
That he succumbed is shown by his friends : the Abbé
Bullinger, Ignaz Parhammer S.J., later Confessor to the
Emperor himself, and other priests. It is clear from his
letters that Leopold Mozart no more doubted his religion
than Englishmen doubt the importance of international
trade. His religion was the religion of everyone he knew.
He held his faith purely, more so perhaps than his neigh-

bours. He was hard, and held it hardly : had he been a
Scotsman, he would have been a dour, Kirk-attending,
Meenister-criticising Puritan. In the Church of England
he would have been restless, and gone either to very
high or very evangelical places of worship.

Salzburgian doings during the period of Wolfgang's
infancy were several. The Neutor tunnel was driven by
the express orders of the Archbishop through the
Monschberg. These almost unreal and in some ways
and in some lights " aweful " earthworks, fortresses and
natural cliffs seem to emit the string fugato announcing
the Duet of the Two Men in Armour. Less Gothic in
the Romantic sense was the substitution of a rococo
for a formal four-sided spire on St. Peter's (compare the
strange steeples on Southwell Minster), substantially
helping to give present-day Salzburg its well-known
silhouette. The heavy Pauline look was added to the church
in the Makartplatz, as it is now, then the Hannibalplatz.

Disappointingly refusing to be conscious of the
possibilities of his own city, Leopold Mozart had nothing
which would have pleased Horace Walpole in the volume
which Lotter of Augsburg printed in 1759, *Der Morgen
und der Abend*, in which Eberlin's music joined with
Leopold's to furnish material for the mechanical Hornwerk on the fortress walls : distressingly matter-of-fact
stuff, very similar in style to simple keyboard music.

The general style of the Hornwerk is that of a volume
of sonatas which had recently been published in Nuremberg and which Leopold Mozart had in his flat, and which
his little boy Wolfgang had early heard and learnt from.
These sonatas [E1] contained examples by Galuppi,
Rutini and Sammartini, and were therefore really cem-
balo music, though later volumes from Nuremberg

introduced real clavichord sonatas by C. P. E. Bach, whose influence on Wolfgang was not only direct but even more powerful as heard through the music of that apt imitator, Wolfgang's father. Consider this C. P. E. Bach-like opening of a sonata in F by Leopold Mozart:

or this, from a sonata in C:

or this forward looking music from the same work:

When not influenced by C. P. E. Bach, Leopold Mozart's style was usually modelled on the Italian violin school as exemplified by such Germans as Biber. This opening of a Divertimento, with its arresting forte, and its subsequent piano semiquaver figure, is typical [S 28]:

Openings apart, so often the equivalent of the premier coup d'archet, what is a Leopold Mozart melody like?

This melodic line was composed in August 1762 in a concerto for solo trumpet, perhaps written for the Court trumpeter, Andreas Schachtner, with horns, strings and a figured bass. As an example of Leopold Mozart's pleasant, naïve writing—

the above shows his love of the echo effect. The passage for two horns is marked " piu tosto (a gusto d'un eco) un poco allegretto."

Other music which influenced Wolfgang was that of
Michael Haydn. At this time (during our First Period,
1756 to the February of 1762) Michael Haydn was still
in the service of the Bishop of Grosswardein [D3], but
he was writing a Te Deum which Wolfgang was later
to follow very closely [E1] in K 141.

The last full year in which the whole Mozart family
of four members, that is to say, father, mother, daughter
and son, were in Salzburg, showed them well established
and with an influential circle of friends, some of whom
have already been mentioned. Besides the ecclesiastics,
professional men and the steadier sort of musicians, their
friends included their landlord, Lorenz Hagenauer, who
owned the whole of the house, now No. 9 Getreidegasse,
his wife Maria Theresa, and their daughters Ursula and
Francesca.

Leopold Mozart used a music copyist named Estlinger ;
when Frau Mozart shopped in the Getreidegasse she
visited the establishments of Reifenstuhl, Zezi and Frank
Xaver Gschwendner Kerschbaumer in the Marktplatz[1]
and, in the Judengasse, Freysauf. Their favourite
churches were St. Clara (Loreto), that dedicated to The
Holy Child, that of S. Francesco di Paola and the beautiful
white building on its hill named St. Maria Plain. Wolfgang loved a drive, and this three-mile journey to the
hill gave him great pleasure. Activities in which the
family could join with friends became increasingly
pleasurable as Wolfgang grew older, card-playing and a
game at shooting with air guns at comic drawings
M 19-20
.

But music filled his infancy, indeed, it did this whether

---

[1] Not the same as the present-day name Makartplatz, named after a painter
named Makart, a square on the other side of the Salzach.

he liked it or not. His older sister was taught her notes in this confined upper flat, his father was busy composing and giving violin lessons, and visitors combined with his father in chamber music. Little Wolfgang was attracted magnetically to the keyboard : not really a surprising thing, most babies are, crawling across the room to climb up the legs to press damp and sticky hands on the white keys, wondering at the ensuing noise. But Wolfgang soon did more, he began to pick out thirds. His father, turning aside a little from teaching his daughter, helped Wolfgang, who absorbed information so quickly that he could play when he was 4 and compose when he was 5. Both activities were limited : the first by the stretch of his hand, and the second by his inability to write. The earliest of these minuets which his father wrote down and carefully preserved are printed in various places, on page 14 of Wyzewa and St. Foix, ₂and on page 7 of Holmes's *Life* W 4 and H 3. None of this music seems to me to have any aesthetic interest. Wolfgang was by no means the only child prodigy of his century, and if any musicologist thought it worth while to compose a thesis on the subject of music written before the age of 7, by Mozart, the two Wesley boys, the little Crotch and others, there is no certainty that he would pick out Wolfgang as different in kind. Among prodigies he was merely a prodigy : it is among men that he is unique.

Nissen, Wolfgang's wife's second husband, recounts a story presumably given in the first place by Nannerl, and to be found in all the biographies. It tells how Leopold, back from playing in some Cathedral service, and mounting the stairs with a friend, found Wolfgang in the middle of the composition of a piano concerto, the MS. so full of blots as to be scarcely legible. Schachtner recounts an incident in which little Wolfgang was unhappy at being left out of a string trio in which Wenzl, Schachtner himself and Leopold took part. Little Wolfgang, to keep him quiet, was allowed to double Schachtner's part, but he played so well that Schachtner ceased playing, Wolfgang taking the whole part over.

When it was bed-time, Wolfgang would stand on a chair and sing with his father " Oragna fiagata fa." The boy would then kiss his father on the top of his nose and say that when he was a man he would put his father in a glass case to protect him from the draughts [M 18]. Besides " Oragna fiagata fa," Wolfgang used the verbally meaningless music of the syllables " Nannetta Nanon, puisue la bedetta fa, Nannetta, inevenedetta fa Nanon " [M 25]. His love for this verbal nonsense grew until it became one of his main characteristics as an adult letter-writer. One may see in these letters an exploitation to an unusual degree of a natural human pleasure in speaking sounds which only contain the vaguest literary meaning. This sort of volubility in which meaning is guessed rather than known is rhythmic, musical and suggestive, and did not receive further exploitation than that which Wolfgang Mozart gave it until the times of Lewis Carroll, Edith Sitwell and James Joyce.

Except when excited by music, Wolfgang was a " good " baby, affectionate, biddable and liking travel. All his life he continued affectionate, making friends easily, and his spirits always rose in a fast post-chaise. Third to music and to travel, he enjoyed arithmetic.

Watching and listening was his father. Leopold Mozart perhaps now lived through the happiest years of his life : his prodigy of a son, his dear wife, his talented daughter, his hopes for preferment to the post of Vice-Kapellmeister, buttressed by his deep Catholic faith, gave him all save money that he needed from life. At the " Contentamento " he wrote in a notebook, which had better be described in the next chapter, this chapter may close:

# 2

# The Second Salzburg Period

## SIX YEARS OLD

*Residence :*     Flat in the Löchelplatz
*Archbishop :*    Schrattenbach

AFTER A SHORT visit to Munich, by February 1762 the Mozarts were all back home, where they remained until the following September. Then they all set out on their first really great adventure : a visit to Vienna to show off the two children in the capital. The Munich visit, which divides the First and Second Periods, was a less ambitious affair, and Wolfgang returned from his performances before the Elector of Bavaria not noticeably changed.

The events of this Second Period were few, but important. Eberlin died on 21st June, but this did nothing to improve Leopold Mozart's position. But as his mind was now on the genius of his son and on the projected Vienna tour, he was not unduly restless at the lack of promotion. He secured a deputy for his teaching job in the Choir School, giving this deputy all his pay. This cautious and reasonable action is typical of Leopold at this time : some men, more sanguine of the future, would have resigned the work outright, others, more mean, would have attempted at least a little profit, as indeed he himself would have done towards the end of the story.

But the chief event of all was the arrival in Salzburg of Michael Haydn, younger brother by four years of Joseph Haydn ; he came from the Court of Bishop Count Firmian of Grosswardein. Archbishop Schrattenbach, whose nephew the Bishop of Grosswardein was, welcomed Michael Haydn, and appointed him " conductor " of his Court orchestra. This means that he sat at the harpsichord, filled in the figured bass and kept the players together. It does not mean that he supervised, let us say, the phrasing and bowing of the strings, far less does it mean he chose the programmes ; the imposing title meant subordination both to the Kapellmeister and the Vice-Kapellmeister. It would appear, however, that Michael Haydn was appointed to a position senior to that which Leopold held at that time. Michael Haydn's pay was 300 florins, not so bad for a young man of 25, being about fifty pounds or one hundred and forty dollars. One may assume the cost of living in Salzburg was less than that of England because the latter country was wealthier and therefore money was less scarce. England's cost of living had risen in the previous century, especially in London. I think it fair to relate Salzburg in 1762 to London of a hundred years back. Two years before this date (1662) Samuel Pepys, aged 28, married and with a small establishment in Axe Yard, Westminster, was paid £50 per annum for his official duties, and he could save money on it.

Dittersdorf was offered Michael Haydn's position at Grosswardein, which was that of a singularly influential Kapellmeister, at 1,200 gulden (£120) with free board and lodging and with maintenance and livery for a

servant [D3].   There may therefore be some evidence
that Michael Haydn left an excellent position in a small
and unbalanced Bishopric for a subordinate but safer
position in a much larger and better run Archbishopric—
though we perhaps must not be quite certain that Dittersdorf is always accurate.   He wrote when he was old and
unhappy.   Again, Dittersdorf, whom the Bishop was
most anxious to secure, may have been offered terms
which would have dazzled Michael Haydn.   But time
has shown that Michael Haydn was fortunate in leaving
Grosswardein, a diocese within the Kingdom of Hungary
and not possessing nominal sovereign independence like
Salzburg, for the Bishop fell into disgrace with Maria
Theresa, and his musical establishment had to be closed
down.   It happened like this : one of Maria Theresa's
regiments was stationed in the diocese, and its Colonel,
who was only 27, was very fond of music and dancing.
His Adjutant sang basso profondo.   Another Colonel's
daughter was very beautiful.   The Adjutant, several
junior officers and the girl enjoyed diverting amateur
dramatics.   They even sang operas.   One day the Bishop
held an open air procession headed by " Turkish "
music, which was then becoming very fashionable and
which was to fascinate Wolfgang Mozart.   This flaunting
of secular high spirits was noted by a subordinate ecclesiastic and was reported to Maria Theresa.   Her Private
Secretary wrote to the Bishop that he had been accused
of having had operas performed in his own private
theatre during Lent and of supporting scandalous open
air processions.   Consequently, as was only fair, Her
Majesty proposed to send a Commission to Grosswardein
to inquire into the allegation.

In haste the worried Bishop dismissed everybody,

including Dittersdorf. All this would become known in Salzburg, giving Michael Haydn cause to reflect that it was better to serve a Prince-Archbishop than a Bishop, and giving Schrattenbach much secret amusement.

During the six or seven months which constitute this Second Period, Wolfgang continued under his father's tuition. He wrote out for his son both original music and transcriptions from C. P. E. Bach and others, arranged in twenty-five suites and bound together in an album <sup>M 14</sup>.

When the Mozart family left Salzburg for Vienna in September, they left their empty flat in the charge of their landlord, Lorenz Hagenauer. Then for some months Salzburg knew nothing of them, the first hint of their return being Hagenauer's order to the porter to have their stove lighted for a few hours to air the place. He had had this request from Vienna in a letter dated 29th December 1762.

# 3

## The Third Salzburg Period

### PRE-LONDON TOUR

Residence :       Flat in the Löchelplatz
Archbishop :   Schrattenbach

THIS PERIOD EXTENDS from their return from
the Court at Vienna on the 5th January 1763 until the
9th June in the same year. In Vienna the two children
had delighted the Emperor Francis, the Empress Maria
Theresa and the archdukes and archduchesses, their
children. When they left Salzburg once again after a
brief stay of five months, they stopped away for years,
for this tour was to be the longest of all and was to
include, for the first and only time, London.

The Third Period opened auspiciously, for Leopold
gained his ambition. He was promoted Vice-Kapellmeister on 28th February 1763 [E 1]. There was a new
Kapellmeister at last, in place of the defunct Eberlin,
in the person of an Italian, Giuseppe Francisco Lolli,
of Bologna, who had for some time been assisting
Eberlin. Adlgasser, the pupil of Eberlin, and so much
the favourite of Schrattenbach's predecessor, seems to
have received no new appointment, and cannot have
loved Lolli more than the Mozarts. The only drawback
to Leopold Mozart's elevation was that he came to
expect the Kapellmeistership itself in due course. Lolli
had succeeded Eberlin, might not Mozart succeed Lolli?

Wolfgang, at no time self-conscious, was not changed in character by his great Viennese success. He continued to find his chief friends among musicians, and the boy preferred the society of Wenzl, Hebelt and Vogt the violinists, Deible the oboist, Leutgeb the horn player, Spitzeder the tenor singer and clavier teacher, and of Adlgasser himself, while Adlgasser's assistant, Lipp, was at this time more at home in the Mozart circle than he was to become later. About the only young woman in Wolfgang's circle when a small boy was Rosalie Joly, chambermaid to Count Arco and nicknamed Sallerl: she was a friend of Nannerl's.

The Hagenauers were not only of use to Leopold as kindly landlords and trustworthy friends, but included among their relations interesting people who enriched the Mozarts' circle of acquaintances. Cajetan Hagenauer entered the monastery of St. Peter: in due course, twenty-two years later, he became its Abbot. Wolfgang was to write Masses to celebrate Cajetan's several steps in the novitiate. Johann Baptist Hagenauer, a distant relation but a particular protégé of Lorenz, was appointed Court Sculptor and Inspector of Galleries to the Archbishop: he married an Italian portrait painter, Rosa Barducci.

By the time Cajetan had entered the monastery and Johann had married, the Mozarts were off on their long journeys which occupied them until 1766, and while they travelled through the Low Countries, France and England, it is of interest to note what political changes were occurring round them.

Joseph, the eldest son of the Emperor Francis and of Maria Theresa, was as musical as his mother, being a good harpsichord player and accompanist from a figured bass, surely a real test of musicianship. While the Mozarts were away he became King of the Romans, which means he was accepted by the Electors of the Empire as Heir Apparent to the Imperial Throne, and the year before the Mozarts returned, the Emperor Francis had visited Innsbruck for the marriage of his second son, the Archduke Leopold. During the performance of an opera there one afternoon, the Emperor, feeling unwell, left the theatre, fell into the arms of the King of the Romans, and forthwith died of apoplexy. This event, and the consequent automatic accession of Joseph as Emperor took place on 18th August 1765, and it took eight days for the news to reach the Mozarts as they passed through Lille on their way to The Hague. This change of Emperor affected Wolfgang later when he left Salzburg for ever to take up freelance work in Vienna, for Joseph was to give him a small Court appointment.

On this tour Wolfgang got smallpox and nearly died : it was ironic that it was exactly at this time that inoculation was first introduced by Maria Theresa, who had a party of children up to Schonbrunn for the purpose.

Ecclesiastically, there was tremendous trouble, for it was during this tour that the Jesuits were expelled from so many countries. In Paris, when the Mozarts were there, the Archbishop of Paris was expelled by Louis XV for trying to protect the Jesuits. Maria Theresa, firm Catholic though she was, was adamant in getting rid of them from her Hapsburg dominions. This enmity towards the Jesuits extended only to the Order, not to the individuals, some of whom remained as private Confessors in their capacity of Priests : but it did mean it was safe to laugh at them, as in *Figaro*.

3b Nannerl married

3a Frau Mozart

Giov: Michele Haydn

4b Michael Haydn

4a Frau Hagenauer

# 4

## The Fourth Salzburg Period

### POST-LONDON TOUR

*Residence* :    Flat in the Löchelplatz
*Archbishop* :   Schrattenbach

THE MOZARTS RETURNED from their long tour
on the 30th November 1766 and did not leave their
flat until the 11th September of the year following : ten
months of rest after accidents and illnesses. The long and
courageous journey had slightly changed their inward
relationships. Wolfgang was by now obviously superior
in musical ability to his sister. Leopold, though worried
about the future as usual, had enough money to think of
renting a whole house. The death of grandmother
Anna Maria Mozart of Augsburg took place when they
had been back home less than a fortnight, and though
Leopold had his worries over his mother's will, he may
well have felt a little easing of his constant anxiety. He
walked in Salzburg in his new English red-brown suit
rather more cheerfully.

Musically, the most important part of their baggage
was a clavichord, the same instrument which is still
housed in the Getreidegasse flat, now the Museum. Its
existence is a matter of some importance : Mozart's
early sonatas, especially those which he was to write in

E

Salzburg such as K 279–83, can be given a " clavichord "
rendering on the pianoforte with some historic justifica-
tion and much musical pleasure, which is perhaps more
to the point. The gradations of tone and interplay of
parts may be treated as though the music was written
for a string quartet, instead of for the noisier and less
sensitive harpsichord. " Clavichord " piano playing
indeed is nothing else than quiet, legato but otherwise
quite ordinary playing, with restrained use of the pedal.
The " pearly Bach touch " loved of some pedagogues
must be avoided, the sudden contrasts of piano and forte
of the harpsichord are equally incongruous, and the
colour effects and sonority of the pianoforte must be
forgone. What Mozart liked above all was the pianoforte, but there does not seem to have been an instrument
of this description in the flat at this time. Mozart in
several places has condemned speed for its own sake, and
the weight of evidence is, that at least the series K 279–83
should be played more slowly and less brilliantly than is
customary, and with greater attention to phrasing and
what play of inner parts the somewhat spare score allows.

This portable clavichord was bought on the outward
journey at Augsburg, from J. A. Stein, and it was used
for practising during the journeys. It long remained a
favourite and years later, when Wolfgang was alone in
Paris with his mother, his father wrote to beg him to get
a clavichord, if he could find one in Paris, as he was so
much more at home with this instrument than with a
harpsichord. Kapellmeister Rust left behind him on
leaving Salzburg a better clavichord than that in the
Mozarts' flat, and Wolfgang wished to have it on his
second return from Paris in 1778. Unfortunately the
instrument was taken over by Rust's successor in the

same lodgings, Ferlendis the oboe player. But this incident shows Wolfgang's continued love for the clavichord as such.

For the first time, Wolfgang's compositions are important enough to mention : his earliest pieces being exercises showing no personality but mere precocity. London had influenced the little boy even more than other cities, because in it lived J. C. Bach, the youngest son of J. S. Bach. J. C. Bach had settled as an opera composer and teacher of the harpsichord, and had written, besides operas, a number of successful keyboard sonatas. In fact, one of the answers to the question, " Who taught Mozart ? " might well be, " J. C. Bach." They were together in London from November 1764 until July 1765, and their musical intimacy was such that the boy transformed some of his mentor's sonatas into harpsichord concertos.

Therefore the nine-year-old Wolfgang who returned, plus travelling clavichord, to Salzburg was already showing signs of difference from other prodigies, for he was growing as much mentally as he was in musical gymnastics. As his active brain reached out for other models, the influence of J. C. Bach began to diminish. During this period of less than a year in the Löchelplatz he manufactured several harpsichord concertos from the works of French sonata writers, not from Couperin or from Rameau, whose style was no longer fashionable, but from composers whose names, except that of Schobert, are completely forgotten by all except specialists. This French style was to influence Wolfgang no longer than did that of J. C. Bach, but how early we may notice his delight in the concerto, with its freedom of form and capacity for drama.

More important musically than these early concertos are two religious works, the first of their sort which he wrote : *Die Schuldigkeit des ersten Gebotes* and a Passion Cantata.

These works did not differ in style, for he had not acquired any feeling for religious emotion. If a greater parallel will not be misunderstood, his outlook was still Haydnesque, meaning by this the mature Joseph Haydn of twenty or more years later, a composer who throughout his life took refuge from the complex questions in the simpler ones of physical description. Even in his greatest religious work, which surely is the *Seven Words from the Cross*, in setting the *I Thirst*, Haydn takes the purely physical image of Christ seeking water from his mother (compare the motif of No. 3 with that of No. 5 : John xix, 26–7 with 28) and his anguish when the soldiers offer gall and vinegar. Nothing could be more appropriately grievous to the hearts of the worshippers in Cadiz Cathedral than this, and it is very far from the case that Mozart was at this time anywhere at all in the same musical realm as Joseph Haydn. It is fairer to say that Haydn at his most naïve (in the *Creation*, perhaps) was still far more sophisticated and powerful than the boy Mozart. But it is this pictorial sort of religious music, " Sunday School music," which interested Wolfgang, and any reference in the text of either the Passion music or the oratorio which could be painted, surely was painted. As for his musical powers, they were already sufficient for him to share with Adlgasser and Michael Haydn the task of writing some of this religious music.

In the Latin play, *Apollo et Hyacinthus*, Wolfgang did not attempt characterisation, and probably did not even realise that there was such a thing. Instead he introduced word painting of the kind he used in religious music. Owing to the Salzburg Puppet Theatre, this music still survives.

Köchel numbers 67 to 69 are the first of an important series of Organ Sonatas, as they are usually called. They were written to please the Archbishop, for the playing of a piece of instrumental music in which the organ had a figured bass part helped the musical worshipper to get from the Gloria to the Credo without the stupefaction of attending to the priest. The practice came to be copied in other Salzburg churches. As the organ only enters as a background, and as the melodic interest is carried by two violins and sometimes by a much larger orchestral grouping, it would be better to call them Epistle sonatas, for that is what they were called by their creator, *sonate all'epistola*. K 67 is an Andante in E flat, in binary form but without repeats, or else it would take too long. It has an appealing melody which in the fifth bar makes effective use of relative minor harmony. K 68 and 69 are both quick movements in sonata form with repeated expositions and short development sections. They are both fairly impressive, in a stately way, but the music is of such a nature that if the organ part were excluded and perhaps violas added, they could both be played with comedy nuances, and would make effective overtures in the opera house. The aesthetic and religious problem which all the Epistle sonatas raise is considered during the Eleventh Period, which deals with the Epistle sonata in C major, K 329, the High Priest of the series. Leopold as well as Wolfgang wrote Epistle sonatas, and so did Michael Haydn.

This musician married Maria Magdalena Lipp, the daughter of the second Cathedral organist, when the

Mozarts were in Vienna in 1768. This marriage displeased them. Nannerl objected to the bride as belonging to a vulgar set. Leopold mocked at the bride's father as being an incompetent musician. Frau Mozart remembered the gossip that the bridegroom had been flirting with a Viennese lady only too recently.

There is a plaque on the house on the right as one ascends the fortress hill after leaving the Cathedral which informs the passer-by that this was where Michael Haydn lived, though the actual house he and his wife inhabited has been pulled down, and another built.

# 5

## The Fifth Salzburg Period

### PRE-ITALIAN TOUR

*Residence :*     Flat in the Löchelplatz
*Archbishop :*    Schrattenbach

ON THE 5th JANUARY 1769 the Mozarts arrived back from Vienna, with the MS. score of *La Finta Semplice* among the luggage. They were to remain in Salzburg until 12th December 1769. *La Finta Semplice* (there are two *La Finta*'s in Mozart's output, so no shortening is possible) is only one of two operatic pieces which he wrote while in Vienna, the other, *Bastien and Bastienne*, does not appear to have been performed in Salzburg. But *La Finta Semplice* was sung before the Archbishop in the Residenz, in that noble apartment with the baroque porcelain stove.

The life of the Mozarts was one of constant bustle. No sooner had they climbed the stairs up to their flat, with their servant[1] left below to deal with the luggage, than there were fresh things to do : in this case, rehearsals for *La Finta Semplice* and a Mass to be written for the start of an early Lent. This proved to be the Missa Brevis in D minor, K 65, sung in the University Church

---

[1] She had a girl friend who later married one of the wealthy Haffners : this made Leopold laugh.

to open the forty hours' prayer; as a Lenten Mass the
Gloria would be omitted, though in fact Wolfgang
composed music for it.

While his son was busy composing and rehearsing,
the father's mind was busy with promotion, money and
the Archbishop. He had already received intimation that
Schrattenbach allowed him to remain in Vienna as long
as he wished, provided he did not want to be paid during
his absence. To show the growing power of the Italians
in the Salzburg Court it may be mentioned that the letter
conveying this cheap permission was written by the
Archbishop's Chamberlain in that language [W4]. But
a point of character in Leopold is, that he showed no
gratitude to Schrattenbach. After all, the Archbishop
made it plain that he deemed Leopold still to be in his
service, so that he always had a home, employment of
some dignity and an income to return to each time he
wandered off with his son, daughter and wife. Leopold
always nourished a grudge against whatever Lord he
served, and it may not have occurred to him that any
gratitude was due for so customary an arrangement.
Certainly the courtesy extended by Schrattenbach to
Leopold was not exceptionally extended, for Joseph
Meisner, for instance, was also absent, and neither
Schrattenbach nor his successor Colloredo ever actually
dismissed a Kapellmeister (Wolfgang never rose to this
rank in the Salzburg service), even though at one time
he had, what with illness and absence, no less than four
on his books. As Leopold was in fact looking round for
some wealthy noble to offer a sufficient inducement to
the Mozarts to settle elsewhere, Schrattenbach was not
without a certain magnanimity.

Leopold, now as in the future, carefully concealed his

search for more remunerative employment. Both in his letters to his landlord while he was away, and in one he wrote to the Archbishop when he had been back a couple of months, he declares that he was detained in Vienna against his wishes, and stopped there for the honour of Salzburg. For instance, when *La Finta Semplice*, written in Vienna, could not after all be produced there, Leopold thought it was his duty to stay in the capital until it could in some other way be proved that his son was a competent composer. This proof was afforded by Father Parhammer, the Jesuit friend of former days, who com-missioned Wolfgang to write a Mass for the opening of an orphanage : though the Society of Jesus had been proscribed, many Jesuits were still held in high esteem; the Emperor himself was among the congregation. Thus Wolfgang, who conducted his Mass personally, had the amplest opportunity to impress Vienna, and did so very successfully. Leopold therefore no longer feared that Vienna was laughing at him about the withdrawal, unperformed, of *La Finta Semplice*, and, failing to find the hoped-for preferment, the family returned to Salz-burg. However, owing to some defect in the Salzburg bureaucracy, he received no pay for a few months after his return even when he was indeed performing the duties of his office as Vice-Kappellmeister, and no doubt suffered a little anxiety. So he wrote to the Archbishop in March for this pay, and secured it.

Besides the Parhammer Mass for Vienna, Wolfgang also wrote one for his old friend Cajetan Hagenauer, who, four or five years ago, used to blow the organ for him, fetch him his air gun and often catch flies for him [M 19]. Now Cajetan was Father Dominicus in the Monas-tery of St. Peter, and about to celebrate the first Mass

of his new priesthood. K 66, the " Pater Dominicus,"
was conducted by Wolfgang with a baton in the gallery
of the church, for while conducting from the harpsichord
was the method for opera, time beating (rather than
conducting) was the convention in the German-speaking
lands at this time for Church music. K 66 is of some
importance historically, with its occasional symphonic
orchestral predominance, but the general operatic
nature of its solos remained, and was a feature which
never completely departed from Mozart's Church music
while he lived in Salzburg.

In the short period between his return from his
London tour, and setting out for Italy, Mozart wrote
little besides these two Masses except a Cassation
in G (K 63) which alone might be worth rehearsing
to-day.

To his circle of friends Wolfgang added Cirillus
Hofmann, a dancing master, whom he later had in mind
when writing a contredanse K 123 ᵂ⁴. His first known
letter dates from this period : it is to a girl, and is a little
pedantic, like the Pater Dominicus, as though Wolfgang
seemed likely to turn out a second Leopold. An important new friend was Sigmund Robinig, son of G. J.
Robinig of Rottenfeld. Joachim Ferdinand von Schieden-
hofen who later became Court Councillor was another
influential addition ᴹ¹⁸. Among the musicians, the
brothers Schulz, both bassoon players, became favourites.
The ease with which Wolfgang made friends, especially
with those whom a young boy often finds most difficult,
boys older than himself, makes his later strong dislike of
Salzburg all the more poignant; it shows how stifled
he felt musically, although he had so many delightful
friends.

Wolfgang began to learn Latin and was given a titular appointment by Schrattenbach of Konzertmeister. This post later became more active, but as at this time it demanded no work, perhaps it was but fair that Wolfgang received no pay either.

Thus in learning Latin, playing with friends, writing Latin Church compositions and a few secular instrumental ones, living in a flat where clothes were hardly unpacked before they were packed again, while his father walked up and down meditating the long projected tour to Italy, Wolfgang's fourteenth year passed away.

His father paid much attention to, and derived comfort from, the presence of such physical objects as crucifixes, and complains on his travels when the inns at which he stops are too Protestant in tone to have such ornaments or reminders of faith. If we may judge from the extant letters, Leopold was not a student of the Bible, and his attendances at Mass were mainly professional. Yet his mind was deeply coloured with such religious ideas as had found suitable soil there, and his friendships with Father Parhammer and the Abbé Bullinger kept those religious ideas current in his time and place, alive in his soul. Of these, that which finds most frequent expression in his letters, and which most influenced his character and therefore his life and the life of his son, was that expressed to Lorenz Hagenauer in a letter from Vienna written before the return to Salzburg with which this chapter deals. " Fiat voluntas tua " he quotes, and adds " What God does not want, I do not want either " M 19. With Don Ottavio, Leopold would indeed say " Convien chinare il ciglio al volere del ciel " but unlike that amiable nincompoop could never look around for any " dolce compenso " the situation might afford.   Leopold indeed had more of Donna Anna in his composition.

This interpretation of " Thy Will be done " was always his.   It is the most disciplinary and least alive of those possible.   Balked in his ambitions as he constantly was, he submitted to events in a sort of surly wounded self-abasement which was really quite against his own lively, ambitious and enterprising nature.   Had he been able to interpret " Thy Will be done " as an expression of deter-  .  mination on the part of the petitioner, that the qualities of heavenly love would be manifested, as far as the petitioner was able, in his life that day, allied, in fact, to " give us this day our daily (spiritual) bread," he would have been less rebellious and found it easier to be com-fortable in Salzburg.   It is unlikely that such a change in his disposition would ever have brought him the coveted Kapellmeistership because it is fairly clear that in the opinion of both Schrattenbach and Colloredo, his successor, the only suitable holder of such an office was an Italian.   But the Vice-Kapellmeistership, and his teaching connections and his excellent reputation for sobriety, good sense, learning and education, his success-ful book, his happy home life, his wonderful son and talented daughter, should have been capable of rounding off an unusually happy and successful life, which pro-gressed from the orphaned bookbinder's son to the solid, strong and intellectual Salzburg musician and citizen.

That he was aware of his rise in the world is evident in a letter in which he asks his wife and son if his careful thought of money and the future were not justified, for look, he seems to say, at the difference between my poor brothers and myself !   This attribution of his success neither to the goodness of Providence nor to his musical abilities made his psychological disposition all the more dangerous to the happiness of his family : intrigue had worked before, and it would surely work again [M18].

Another interpretation of *Fiat voluntas tua* is the more positive construction of the need for an attempt by the supplicator experimentally to discover the *voluntas* from trial and error. This is Panglossian and can be as easily covered with ridicule by innumerable Voltaires as the impressive advice of Job's Comforters can be covered with abuse. Nevertheless, Pangloss and the Comforters do in fact often score heavily in worldly things. Pangloss would have accepted the failure of *La Finta Semplice* in Vienna, saying it was all for the best, as the future would undoubtedly show. The consequent performance of the Parhammer Mass before the Emperor and the Court would have shown that, in this case, all might well be for the best, for here Leopold saw his son conduct, baton in hand, a Mass of his own composition, written in the most fashionable taste, and convincing the noble congregation that his son was an accomplished musician. But who knows what fiasco might have attended *La Finta Semplice* in the opera house ?

However absurd Pangloss may be, his attitude makes for resilience and opportunism, but Leopold, whose character and life surely makes us love him, chose the cold, the rigorous view of his favourite *Fiat voluntas tua*, and even, later, approached the point of view that, just as he had to accept innumerable denials from his heavenly father, so, in his turn, should his son Wolfgang receive as many denials of his wishes from his earthly father. The earthly son broke loose from his earthly father : did not Leopold ever wish to break loose from his heavenly father ? Wolfgang escaped into the sunlight of

the moral conceptions voiced in *The Magic Flute*, but
Leopold never knew an alternative to his strict Roman
Catholicism, and to the family in the Löchelplatz
Voltaire was a mad dog, even though perhaps at that
very time their own Archbishop to be, Colloredo, was
reading and enjoying his works.  In the local air of
Salzburg, Leopold became more holy than the Pope, and
the local Pope did not like him any the better for it.

On the 12th December 1769, Leopold and his son left
together for Italy, travelling from Salzburg along the
Innsbruck road.  They stopped at Worgl, the railway
station of which is sometimes a stop of the Orient Express
to-day, and the address on the letter shows that the wife
and daughter were staying with their landlord :

> A Madame
> Madame Marie Ane
> Mozart a Salzbourg
> in der Traidgasse
> ben H. Lorenz
> Hagenauer

The mixture of languages is very typical.

Nannerl had an exciting time at home and with the
Hagenauers while her brother astonished Italy.  She was
wooed by a son of a Court Chancellor, Felix von Molk,
but she did not marry the young man, Anton Joseph by
name.  The number of her flirtations, and subsequently
her duality of husbands, suggest a charming and attractive girl.  She wrote often to her brother, and shared with
him a taste for arithmetic, while he enjoined her to visit
the Mirabell Chapel for the sake of the music there.  Both
Nannerl and her mother had their portraits painted, and
kept up their large circle of friends.  Every now and then

the post would bring some demand from Leopold which would make them search out a copy of his *Versuch* or a coat left behind by mistake. In their turn, they would tell him the Salzburg gossip, a daughter born to the Michael Haydns, the departure of Joh. Kaspar Kostler, the trumpeter ; but they never mentioned international news. They did not suppose that the meetings between the Emperor and the King of Prussia could concern them, however ominous these meetings were for Poland and might be for the peace of Europe. The family of Count Firmian counted for much more, because it was to the Count himself, in his capacity of Chief Steward, that their absent husband and father would be writing for extensions of leave, those applications for extensions which were more and more to be expected from the Vice-Kapellmeister. From time to time a traveller, such as the bass singer Josef Meisner, would return to Salzburg with news and complaints of the inns, but above all there would be the letters from Italy of Lèopold and Wolfgang themselves to amuse their days.

# 6

## The Sixth Salzburg Period

### THE YOUNG ITALIAN

*Residence :*    Flat in the Löchelplatz
*Archbishop :*    Schrattenbach

FATHER AND SON returned from Italy by the same route as their exit from the Province of Salzburg through Innsbruck and Worgl. They reached home on 28th March 1771, and remained there only until 13th August of that year, when once more they set out for Italy. In this four and a half months Wolfgang completed two MSS. he had begun in Italy (K 116 and 118) and then started on a whole number of works, including several symphonies.

One MS., which was unfinished, was an oratorio dealing with Judith (K 118) : this work had only four choruses to its many operatic arias, a fact which separates it from the Handelian type of oratorio. Two of these choruses, especially that in the second part in which Judith herself sings, have an interest for us in the combination of solo voice with chorus.

The influence of Padre Martini of Bologna was felt in some of the Church music. A Kyrie, K 90 (reproduced ᴱ³), is an example. There is MS. evidence that Mozart sat down to write a short piece on what the

Elizabethans called " points " in the Dorian Mode. But the pull of D minor was altogether too strong. As completed, this Kyrie, including a Christe, is a short, possibly *a capella* work, though it is supplied with a figured bass. Fugatos of a few bars each start and terminate, the last of all being modelled on the first, to give the piece eighteenth-century symmetry. Wrought against Mozart's natural way of thinking, this Martini pastiche was as musically barren as much of his Bach and Handel writing was to be later in Vienna. However, all this was necessary as exercise for the composer of the counterpoints in *The Magic Flute*.

For the Whitsun of 1771 he wrote a Regina Coeli, K 108, of which the Ora Pro Nobis, set for soprano solo, is a thing of simple and melodious appeal. Its opening and closing ritornelli alone would give a précis of the whole aria, the vocal part merely repeating and enlarging upon the rounded cantabile beauties. Coming in the middle of a somewhat barren and formal work, it is enchanting, and surprisingly mature.

The symphonies also give the Sixth Period its Italianate air : these were K. Anh 216 in B flat, K 75 in F, K 73 in C, and K 110 in G. However, the influence of Joseph Haydn is discerned by Saint-Foix ; we do not know how Wolfgang came across his music, all we know is, that he had not yet met the man himself. Wolfgang's visits to Vienna and the presence of Michael Haydn in Salzburg are telling conjunctions of fact.

So much, or rather, so little, for the music of this period. Salzburg gossip was unimportant. The child born to the Michael Haydns died. Johannes Hagenauer, son of the landlord, and friend of Wolfgang, flirted with Caterina Wider. J. Baptist Hagenauer, a relation and

F

protégé of the landlord's, was completing the lead
statue of the Virgin still to be seen outside the Cathedral.
Kapellmeister Lolli conducted in the Cathedral with a
baton. The sister of the brother who is flirting with
Nannerl, flirts with Nannerl's brother. Wolfgang
typically names this von Molk, "Waberl," for Anna
Barbara. She was four years older than Wolfgang. At
this time most of his friends were older than himself :
for example, Heinrich Wilhelm von Haffner, of " the "
family. There was, by the way, another Waberl, Barbara
Eberlin, daughter of the late Kapellmeister.

On 13th August the two Mozarts, father and son, left
Salzburg once more for Italy, though this time only as far
as Milan. While they were busy with *Ascanio in Alba*,
events in Salzburg hastened to a crisis, the resolution of
which greatly affected the Mozarts, even, by a chain of
causation, explaining Wolfgang's death at the age of 35.

For some time the Mozarts remained quite ignorant
that their Archbishop was dying, so much so, indeed,
that as late as 16th November, Leopold was considering
the chances, however pessimistically, of Schrattenbach
appointing his son to some paid appointment now that
the Serenata which was the purpose of their visit to
Milan, *Ascanio in Alba*, had been very successful, and
pleased, as he hoped, not only the Archduke and Arch-
duchess but also the Empress Maria Theresa herself.

Typically, Leopold's first action on arriving in Salzburg
and learning of the death of Archbishop Schrattenbach
the day before was to write to Hochwurdig Hochge-
bohrne Herrn Herrn : Herr Domprobst Dombechant,
Senior und gesammt Regierendes DomCapitl des hohen
Erzstifts Salzburg, Hochgnadig und Hochgebietende
Herrn Herrn ! in other words, what we would call the

Dean and Chapter, asking that as the late Archbishop had given him permission to accompany Wolfgang to Italy, who indeed had had to go on the direct orders of Maria Theresa herself, and as the work his son had to do had been achieved with such acclamation, the late Archbishop joining others in his praise, could he, Leopold Mozart, please, have the sum of 59 gulden due to him because . . .

This letter is both comic and pathetic. Leopold had no feeling for Schrattenbach as a man, and there is no reason why he should have had. His journeys involved the expenditure of large sums, much larger than 59 gulden, only about six pounds or sixteen dollars. Although we may smile at Leopold's earnestness, he himself does not seem to have thought that the Domprobst Dombechant, Senior and the rest would have thought him rather menially indifferent. It could have waited.

But as this is the return from Italy, it should belong to the next chapter, and is only included here as a backward Schrattenbach glance, so as to leave the page clear for his more important, in the Mozartian association of the word, successor.

# 7

# The Seventh Salzburg Period

## COLLOREDO'S ENTHRONEMENT

*Residence :*    Flat in the Löchelplatz
*Archbishop :*   Colloredo

THE PERIOD OF Wolfgang's stay in Salzburg called in this book " Colloredo's Enthronement " was from 15th December 1771 until 24th October 1772, when he once more and for the third and last time, left with his father for Italy.

Hieronymus Colloredo not only belonged to a wealthy, noble and influential family, but was the eldest son of an eldest son [c3]. His grandfather had been Governor of Lombardy, and there was an Italian branch of the family, one member at least attaining the rank of Cardinal, residing in Rome and writing charming Italian secular verse.

Hieronymus's father was foremost among those of Maria Theresa's councillors who, compromising between their dignity and conscience on the one hand and their desire to serve the Imperial Court on the other, strove to perform their too limitedly dynastic duties while avoiding intrigue, either for or against the often able favourite of the time. We have already noticed his uncle in the

diplomatic service in London, a younger brother, whose
second wife was a Schrattenbach, was in Paris in the same
service.  A second uncle was a Field Marshal, three of
Hieronymus's brothers attained this rank, and his
sisters married within the nobility, one of them becoming
a Lodron.

Hieronymus, just about forty years of age, was Bishop
of Gurk, when by the death of Schrattenbach the opportunity arose for the Colloredos in both Vienna and in
Rome to suggest Hieronymus as a nominee to the independent and wealthy Prince-Archbishopric of Salzburg
which carried with it the titular Primacy of Germany :
this was not an exclusive claim, other ecclesiastical
monarchs were also Primates.   In addition to these
honours, the Archbishopric of Salzburg carried with it a
Papal Legateship, with strong probability of a Cardinal's
hat later.  Lastly, the appointment did not even require
Hieronymus to relinquish his Diocese of Gurk, where
he could if he wished install a Suffragan, though in fact
he did relinquish Gurk later, before 1778 [M 18].

Therefore through both Imperial and Papal channels
the " Herr Domprobst Dombechant, Senior " and others
were duly notified that they might consider, if they
pleased, the name of the Bishop of Gurk, as a possible
candidate for the Archbishopric, and the Salzburg Dean
and Chapter freely and of their own consent did in fact
vote Hieronymus to be their Archbishop on 14th March
1772.

The relationship between Colloredo and the boy of
genius young enough to be his son, started well.  A
week or so after Colloredo had taken up residence, with
a sister as hostess and housekeeper, he made effective
Schrattenbach's appointment of Wolfgang as Konzert-

meister by granting him the salary of 150 gulden a year, which might be taken as roughly £3 ($8.40) a week in our money to-day. Wolfgang was 15 at the time : not a very good salary, but not a very bad one. Indeed, except for some slight hostility which developed later between Colloredo and the Bishop of Chiemsee, there is no evidence at this time to show that the new Archbishop was in any way particularly difficult to work under.

Wolfgang had to earn his modest stipend, and he wrote a " Theatrical Action in One Act," named *Il Sogno de Scipione* for Colloredo's solemn installation on 29th April and four days following. This installation was like a coronation, and came after the Archbishop's acceptance of effective power on the formal offer by the Dean and Chapter on 14th March.

*Il Sogno* had a libretto by Metastasio, but even so perhaps Colloredo thought it not Italian enough, for he appointed a new Kapellmeister in Fischietti, a composer of opéra bouffe and of oratorio. Lolli seems from this time to fade a little from the picture, but he remained a titular Kapellmeister until his death in Salzburg seven years later.

Fischietti had been Kapellmeister at Dresden, and his arrival may be said to signalise a change in Salzburg's music, a change it is difficult to define, because for twenty years or so it had been modern, freed from the figured bass and the binary form, though using both at times. Sonatas, symphonies and divertimenti had been performed, and even the opera, though it retained both the harpsichord and the da capo aria, had ensemble and a greater musical plasticity than was to be found even in Alessandro Scarlatti, or, as far as *La Serva Padrona* is

applicable, in Pergolesi. For this last Pergolesi comparison, it is enough to instance the mock conjuring aria
in *Bastien and Bastienne* written by Wolfgang in Vienna.
Though this was written in Vienna, it came from the pen
of a Salzburg composer and may thus be called Salzburg
music, and a proof that Salzburg opera was more adapt-
able to characterisation than the Italian opera, even that
of opéra bouffe.

With Fischietti brought in by a musical Archbishop
who valued music as he might value fine cloth or good
wine, begins that Salzburg period often called galant,
a word easy to use but hardly possible to define. What it
is not, is easy : it is not polyphonic. A galant movement
does not teem with ideas, though it may take a long time
repeating one or two ideas. Galant melody is not subtle :
galant emotion is not passionate or tragic. But wit,
pith, the pathetic, the well turned phrase, the sudden
dramatic turn (if well-bred), the delightful melody, the
fitting accompaniment, may or may not be galant. It is
merely that the galant qualities were most sought after,
and " mere " musicianship as little wanted as it was in
cultivated Kensington drawing-rooms in the 1890–1914
period. Depth, romanticism, other-worldliness, philo-
sophy : these things are the opposite of galant but on the
same plane. The romantics call galant music pink ribbon :
Colloredo would have called late romantic music tedious
and ill-bred. Neither extreme cared for music as such.
Wolfgang's nascent genius might have been appreciated
in the Salzburg of Eberlin and Schrattenbach had he
been born ten years earlier than he was. But the new
musical atmosphere which became settled in the 1770's
was as treacherous to his genius as that of the Nordic
and Anglo-Saxon musical atmospheres of the 1890's.

He was too independent in spirit easily to submit to the galant, though he did submit : he was a century after his death to be called the composer of that " mere " music, the K 550 symphony.

The coming of Fischietti was not of course remarked on for its adverse influence at the time : it merely made Leopold Mozart, who still hoped to be a Kapellmeister, somewhat grim, and Michael Haydn, who had been one, drink a little more. It was yet another blow to the German element.

We have spoken of the range of characterisation in *Bastien and Bastienne*, but *Il Sogno* was a step backwards, with only one chorus and no ensemble. Metastasio's verse allows illustration to the musician, but not characterisation. His numerous similes gave his almost as numerous composers the sort of thing Haydn loved to do in *The Creation*, and Wolfgang was still in this elementary stage of music drama.[1]

A month after the departure of the Mozarts for the third Italian visit, which started in October 1772, an unknown Salzburg correspondent wrote to Dr. Burney to give him information about the state of music there, as the Englishman had been unable to visit the Archbishopric but wished to add a note about it to the Appendix of the second volume of his German tour. Dr. Burney tells us that " the archbishop and sovereign of Salzburg is very magnificent in his support of music, having usually near a hundred performers, vocal and instrumental, in his service. The prince is himself a

---

[1] " Elementary stage " : it was elementary of Wolfgang, but this does not mean that Haydn's mature use of these scenic devices, any more than Handel's " darkness " chorus in *Israel in Egypt*, is elementary. Both Handel and Haydn, in some ways more typical of their century than Mozart, brought the business of illustration in some of their works to the height of baroque effectiveness, and Mozart did not choose, and might not have been able, to follow them.

dilettante, and a good performer on the violin : he has lately been at great pains to reform his band, which has been accused of being more remarkable for coarseness and noise, than delicacy and high finishing. The Mozart family were all at Salzburg last summer ; the father has long been in the service of that court, and the son is now one of the band ; he composed an opera at Milan, for the marriage of the Archduke, with the princess of Modena, and was to compose another at the same place for the carnival of this year, though he is now but sixteen years of age. This young man, who so much astonished all Europe by his infant knowledge and performance, is still a great master of his instrument : my correspondent went to his father's house to hear him and his sister play duets on the same harpsichord ; but she is now at her summit, which is not marvellous." Then, quoting as directly as translation allows, Burney gives his correspondent leave to speak for himself : " if I may judge of the music which I heard of his composition, in the orchestra, he is one further instance of early fruit being more extraordinary than excellent."

That this should be written at the close of a period when Wolfgang had been about ten months resident in Salzburg and had written no less than fourteen orchestral works, some of which had in them the seeds of immortality, and all of them as good as any other instrumental music to be heard in Salzburg at the time, is one further instance of a simile being more arresting than just.

He was perhaps Italian at this time rather than German, and the symphony meant to him a light, rapid form made up of fast-slow-fast movements, which at its shortest was but an overture. But the symphonic style of writing was so much in his mind that in Milan, composing for a

castrato motet, he used such orchestral effects as a melody
for viola with semiquaver decorations in a long intro-
ductory passage of twenty-three bars, 3/4, Andante, for
*Tu virginum corona* (*Exsultate, Jubilate,* K 165).

By far the best known to-day of the music of this period
is a sonata for piano duet in D, K 381, though one of the
several Divertimenti has been recorded, and there are a
few scores in print and purchasable besides this Divertimento in D, K 131. The reader can gain some idea of the
music written at this time without having to travel to the
nearest depository of the enormous Mozart Gesellschaft.
We wish to pick out the works written in Salzburg which
have proved to be immortal, to try to show their importance in relation to his total output and to relate his
Salzburg works to those written elsewhere; especially
to those written later in Vienna.

This Seventh Period is, then, essentially a symphonic
one, and the symphonic conception, which I take to be a
way of writing rather than a jogtrot formula, subjugated
his ecclesiastical music and gave breadth to many of his
Divertimenti movements. The Duet Sonata in D, K 381,
seems like a short Italian symphony given a transcription
for piano duet. This is especially the case with the
beautiful second subject of the slow movement, which
calls for 'cellos; it is an irritant to the second player to
find this memorable theme doubled by the first player
two octaves above. The whole of this movement,
inspiration apart, owes a good deal to J. C. Bach's Op. 5,
No. 2, published in London, except that it is beautiful
where J. C. Bach's Andante was only pretty. The last
movement starts in the " chord attack in D " manner so
frequently to be found in J. C. Bach and in the Italians,
while in the first movement there is delightfully piquant

passage-work following on the luminous second subject, which formula Wolfgang will often use again, and more effectively even than Cimarosa who at this time was just of age. Both these sonatas are dated by inference and by allusions in the Mozart correspondence.

The Divertimento in D, K 131, is not mentioned in any letters, and the date on the MS. is our authority for placing it in June 1772. A little march ushers in the first movement, and suggests the approach of the players. This beginning, and even sometimes ending, of a whole composition with a march is one of the differences between a divertimento and a symphony or a violin concerto. Indeed, a symphony whose movements were interspersed with those of a violin concerto, making seven movements in all, would already begin to approximate to a divertimento. When we add a second Trio to the Minuet, and begin with a march, there is only one thing left to do. And that is, to add length without strength : to avoid pregnant themes and to repeat and to dwell on longer and more purely melodic ideas.

The first movement of K 131 is certainly symphonic, and its interest lies largely in the development section, one part of which has downward scale passages of the type used by Beethoven in such a work as the finale of Op. 2, No. 1. There is some use of the opening march theme in the bass under a string tremolo. One of the Minuets is very well known because its opening melody, scored for unaccompanied horns, is not only very fetching in itself, but remarkable for its orchestral colour, and, lastly, the presence of two Trios makes the Minuet horn theme enter as often as the theme of a rondo, which this movement, though in rather staid 3/4, thus tends to resemble.

The catchy tunes of the allegretto and of the last movement of all are the sort of things which Mozart at all times dishes up very appetisingly, but what makes him already a great composer in this Seventh Salzburg Period are such passages as the development of the first movement and portions of the Duet Sonata discussed above.

As a prodigy, he was not after all so very much. It was a century of sophisticated children. He was about five years in advance, at any one time, of those also born in 1756. If we survey the larger field of general music, Mozart in his Seventh Period, aged 16, was the equal of the Mendelssohn of the *Midsummer Night's Dream* overture and the Schubert of *The Erl King*. The difference between Mozart and these two is that he continued to grow with a muscularity of intellect and a spiritual discernment both equal to the same qualities in Bach, while Mendelssohn, like another brilliant young man, Rossini, who wrote the witty and even enrapturing overture to *La cambiale di matrimonio* when only 18, failed to build on the foundations his own genius had laid, and repeated himself with increasing skill and experience, but not with increasing inspiration.

Three Divertimenti, or string quartets, contain music both charming and spirited, but though they may be played by solo strings and may take their place in the history of the medium, technically they lag behind Joseph Haydn. Even such a set as Haydn's Op. 9, which, though written some years before, may have been the latest score which Wolfgang is likely to have seen, has much to teach Salzburg composers. Yet the Mozartian magic hovers, alighting from time to time, as in the development section of the Divertimento in D, K 136, to infuse the texture with that glow of genius which makes us treasure even such an unimportant work. Added to these incipient string quartets were seven symphonies, two Epistle sonatas, a Mass, two Latin hymns, a Litany, some songs to German words for voice and orchestra, a duet sonata and a set of minuets. This was the prodigious output of the months of 1772 spent in Salzburg.

As for the rest of Salzburg news, J. B. Hagenauer, a protégé of their landlord's, gave up his Salzburg position as Court Sculptor to go to Vienna, where he worked for the Emperor. Wolfgang became friendly with the son of the Professor of Law at the University (Schlossgangl von Edelbach), and Sigmund Haffner died. But this last event deserves a paragraph to itself.

Sigmund Haffner was a product of the settled and mercenary eighteenth century. He had many interests, including banking, the issuing of loans somewhat on the lines of our modern building societies, and the importation of goods. As the Archbishops tended to become poorer in cash, the wealthy Salzburg merchants tended to become richer in the same commodity, until with Haffner possessing in cash 200,000 gulden while Archbishop Colloredo had very little, it was natural that loans should be arranged; and on the changing of hands of 100,000 gulden, Haffner procured for his heirs freedom from taxes except for regular annual payments of 26,000 gulden. This colossal sum, equivalent to £26,000 in our day, and in Mozart's day equivalent to 26 years of total salary of a prima donna or first-rate Kapellmeister[1] and, bearing in mind this was a bargain for which Haffner thought it worth while to ask, shows either the very great annual turnover of the Haffner business interests, or the

[1] Compare maximum salaries drawn by Aloysia Weber or Dittersdorf.

excessive profits which an established family business officially backed by a series of monopolies could make. This particular Haffner, though the greatest of the family, is not to us the most important. The " Haffner " Serenade and the " Haffner " Symphony were written for other Haffners.

No member of the Mozart family mentioned in any letter the partition of Poland, and father and son went into Hapsburg territory in Italy without any apparent interest in the extension northwards of the huge family property. Wolfgang had been chosen to write and to supervise the production of *Lucio Silla* for the royal Milanese wedding mentioned by Burney, and the choice of a Salzburg youth to write the music was of course gratifying to the German interest as against the Italian.

So father and son travel out of Salzburg on the Innsbruck road on 24th October 1772, and there we must leave them.

# 8

# The Eighth Salzburg Period

## THE ITALIAN SYMPHONIST

*Residence :*    Flat in the Löchelplatz
*Archbishop :*   Colloredo

ON 15th MARCH, FATHER and son returned from a very successful production of *Lucio Silla*, the prelude to which is a three-movement Italian overture, or short symphony. Leutgeb, the restless horn player and old friend of Wolfgang's, had joined them. The Mozarts returned to their Salzburg duties, the one as Vice-Kapellmeister and his son as paid Konzertmeister ; his salary had to include " commanded " works. The relationship between the Mozarts and the Archbishop had already changed. The previous period had been hopeful : Colloredo had had a one-act opera from Wolfgang at his Installation, and had been gratified by the choice of this young musician of his to compose *Lucio Silla* for the Milanese wedding. The Empress herself had chosen Wolfgang Mozart, and heard direct from Milan of the excellent impression his work had made there. All this was creditable to his master, the Archbishop.

But there was a something damaging the Colloredo-Mozart relationship. Although Colloredo may have

been pleased with the success of *Lucio*, what he really
liked himself was Italian opera written by Italians. Did
he himself not bear an Italian name ? He knew there was
one man in the musical establishment who could never
gratify this pleasure, and that man was his Vice-Kapellmeister. But this, though a long continued muttering
pedal bass to the growing misunderstandings, was the
second cause only. The prime cause was a serious change
which took place in the mind of Leopold Mozart. He
stopped away longer than he either need or should in
Milan, hoping to obtain a position with he for whom
*Lucio Silla* had been written, the Archduke Leopold of
Tuscany, the second son of Maria Theresa, who became
Emperor after Joseph. In order to mask this intrigue
he wrote letters in code to his wife telling her not to
worry, and then, in clear, wrote long accounts of the
agony rheumatism was giving him, and how he could not
travel through the snowy Tyrol during the winter. Leopold always supposed that the Archbishop had his
letters intercepted, and always believed that his code
would be secret. But whether his letters were read or
not, or his code understood or not, or even whether
some in Milan later told Colloredo that his Vice-Kapellmeister was active and far from ill, does not really matter.
Leopold had already implanted in himself a deep distrust
of the Archbishop and a complete lack of satisfaction at
returning to Salzburg. This psychological state made no
difference to the outward man's destiny, for in spite of
all his twistings and turnings he remained Vice-Kapellmeister at Salzburg until his death.

His discontent, and, for I suppose we must use the
word, his deceit, may well have been apparent, for
Leopold Mozart was a good man, God-fearing, pure,

hard-working, honourable and responsible, and on such a character deceit does not sit easily. It is difficult to suppose, when Frau Mozart had to run about Salzburg to see the Chief Steward, the Dean, or the wife of the Chief Chamberlain, that no one thought the poor Vice-Kapellmeister's simply terrible rheumatism rather amusing. This deceit hurt no one except Leopold himself, and did not even hurt him financially : what it did do, was to upset his clear view of things, turn him too much into an intriguer, and made him take for granted that his son would do likewise. The tragedy of Leopold's life was that, attempting to leave Salzburg, he failed ; although he could have been happy there. Moreover, as his son had to leave at all costs in order to save his genius from suffocation, a breach was created between bitter father and reckless son which nothing ever really healed. Wolfgang delighted in the open breach between himself and the authorities of his native city, making his unhappy father's case a good deal worse.

During this short Eighth Period, Mozart wrote a little Church music and great deal of instrumental music, though little of it is played to-day. We shall see that, coming within this period, and to be counted as a Salzburgian work, was the Andretter wedding music written in Vienna as a sort of coda.

The Church music completed was one brief Mass, fully orchestrated, written to please Colloredo, who liked full sound and shortness : his tastes were clearly those of Charles II of England, and Mozart was as able to please his Archbishop as Purcell was to please his King. But we might pause for a moment on this problem : Purcell's Services and Anthems are the staple of Anglican Church music, but Mozart's Masses, especially this Trinity Mass,

G

K 167, though they pleased Colloredo, are not now heard in the Catholic Church.

The Anglicans have a great repertoire in the works of Byrd and his contemporaries, and the Catholics have themselves a great repertoire in the works of Palestrina and his school. But Purcell survives in the face of this, while Mozart does not, even in Salzburg.

In the special case of this Trinity Mass, there were no solo arias, for they had to be cut out to please the Archbishop, or else the Mass would have taken too long. So it was not the operatic nature of the music written for the solo voice in this Mass at least which lead to its supersession—even if the Church music of Purcell could always be cleared from the suspicion of operatic influence, which it cannot. Formally and structurally, the choral Trinity Mass should have been of enduring quality : perhaps the secret of its disuse, and of the disuse of its even less suitable brothers, lies in its late eighteenth-century symphonic idiom. The Handel chorus of the first half of the century sounds more formal and aloof than the symphonic chorus of Mozart, even when Mozart is using strict counterpoint : it is partly the lesser importance of the figured bass, and partly the greater use of the orchestral instruments to colour the musical material in an iridescent sheen instead of the set " registration " of the older type of orchestration as used by Handel. Even the music of Mozart's which still is performed in church, though usually rather as a concert than liturgically, brings this point out: the Dies Irae of the Requiem is almost embarrassingly direct and emotional when heard in this setting.

Of the instrumental music, the form most worked was the symphony, but those in E flat (K 184), D (K 181),

C (K 162) and B flat (K 182) are really Italian overtures, with a quick-slow-quick pattern without breaks, and their MS. scores were among those which Leopold did not give out to be copied as not good enough and as likely later to be superseded by his son's own genius. This shows that the word "symphony" already possessed a dignity which made it imperative that it should represent only the best work of a composer. But this particular composer was fond enough of the E flat symphony, K 184, to use some of the material for the incidental music to *Thamos* composed for Vienna.

The music for *Thamos* is serious in intention, and leads us to the much later *Magic Flute*. *Thamos* was a play written by the Baron Gebler, a Viennese official, and had in it some Freemasonical ideas and symbolism, perhaps the first notions that Mozart had so far come across of the Brotherhood. His father would have been most upset had he realised that such un-Catholic seeds were being sown by the text of a play for which his son was furnishing music from a MS. symphony. Although now 17, Wolfgang was supervised by his father in all his details of life in a way that a British or American boy, used perhaps to staying away from home in a boarding school, or camping with other boys in the summer, would hardly be able to tolerate. Too much supervision for too long means too great an estrangement later on.

Though largely written in Salzburg, this first version of the *Thamos* music was completed in Vienna where it was produced and was later, in 1780, amended for the revival of the play by Schikaneder and his troupe[1] when they visited the theatre in the Hannibalplatz.

---

[1] Einstein says it was Bohm, but the weight of evidence surely points to Schikaneder.

A Viennese acquaintance of the Mozarts came to
Salzburg early in July : although he was a member of the
Mesmer family, at the head of which was he who gave
his name to Mesmerism, he was aspiring to no higher
station in life than that of a cook in the Archbishop's
kitchen. The Mozarts had met this Herr Mesmer in the
garden of a house owned by a lady with the admirable
name of Frau von Posch during a performance of *Bastien
and Bastienne* there. Frau von Posch was a relation by
marriage of Dr. Mesmer, who was responsible for the
performance. When later Wolfgang was to erupt so
violently at the time he had to sit with cooks and valets,
we must remember that the broad social milieu of
musicians ranged in gamut from body servants to their
masters : musicians had to be equally at home in all
environments between these two extremes, and it had
not occurred either to Leopold or yet to Wolfgang there
was anything wrong with this arrangement. Doctors,
lawyers, barbers and poets had exactly the same vague
social gamut to play or to endure, as we see clearly from
the novels and comedies of all European nations : in
the morning you walk in St. James's with a Duke, and
in the afternoon you visit your brother, who is a turner.

The symphonic, Church and stage music of this period
has now been examined. There was some chamber music.
A string quartet in E flat, K 160, begun in Milan and
finished in Salzburg is of little musical importance, but
the quintet K 174, though no masterpiece, already shows
the composer interested in the different timbres of the
violin and viola.

The score has been rearranged so as to make it as
clear as possible that we are close to the Sinfonia Concertante K 364 of 1779, however far away emotionally.

A display piece for two violins with orchestra is a move
away from chamber music. This display piece merely
reminds a listener that this was the sort of thing which
Leopold liked : it was often played to show off his son's
virtuosity with the violin. Many people imagine Wolfgang as perpetually seated at the clavier, usually a pianoforte, sometimes a clavichord, rarely a harpsichord

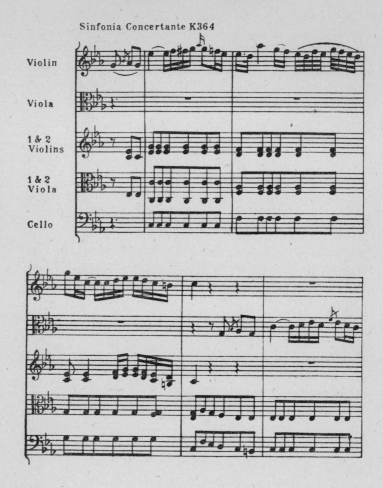

Sinfonia Concertante K364

except at the opera : this is because his pianoforte concertos form the single largest world in his non-operatic
output, and because of pictures and anecdotes dealing
with his Palace or drawing-room improvisations or
contests with other musicians. But the statue in the
market square of St. Gilgen shows him violin in hand, a

position in which he certainly spent most of his musical time as a boy.

The Divertimento in E flat, K 166, is musically the most enjoyable of all his works of this period. It was commissioned in Milan and there started, worked on in the coach on the way back, finished in Salzburg and sent back to Milan to the man who commissioned it.

K 186 in B flat, entirely Milanese, was a sister work, and both were for a wind combination of oboes, clarinets, French horns, English horns and bassoons. Of the two, perhaps the B flat is slightly better known. The Andante grazioso of the E flat is founded on so charming a theme, so perennially delightful an air, that it remains in the memory alongside so many others, but the first of them in time except for the 'cello-like melody of the slow movement of the Duet Sonata discussed in the last chapter.

In spite of the pleasure which much of the music of this period gives, and in spite particularly of the delights of the E flat wind Divertimento, there is no advance on the previous period in musical powers. Wolfgang had already passed his most Italianate point, and it remained in the future for France and for Germany to do their parts in his education.

This period drew to a close when the Archbishop left Salzburg for a tour to Lazenburg, to visit his father at Sierndorf, finishing up with Vienna. The Mozarts, father and son, took the opportunity of slipping off to Vienna themselves. This interrupted some wedding music which Wolfgang was about to write for the son Cajetan of the War Councillor of Salzburg, Andretter.

Hardly had the Mozarts disappeared over the hills, it must have seemed, than music MS. came to Cajetan

Andretter from Vienna, where Wolfgang quickly finished the score.

Though written in Vienna from 21st July, as early as 12th August, Leopold was able to reply to a letter from his wife in which she had told him the Andretter music had been much enjoyed. Wolfgang later had this score posted to him for use in winning over the people of Mannheim and of Paris.

This Andretter wedding serenade, though written in Vienna, was commissioned, then, in Salzburg, and performed there, and may be taken as a coda to this period.

The first movement of this music, given the Köchel number of 185, is a gay allegro assai, into which the knowing read a great deal too much, and the innocent merely kindly good spirits. The second movement introduces the beginning of the usual interspersed violin concerto which, except for a middle section of tautened nerves, is rather empty in a tuneful sort of way. The following slow movement also belongs to this violin concerto, and is formal and rather featureless except for a lambent middle section. Wyzewa and St. Foix discover many indications of the influence of Joseph Haydn in these three movements, though it is one of distribution of material rather than of general feeling, for the music has none of Haydn's melodic, harmonic or cadential characteristics. Much more typical of Mozart's greatest contemporary is the first trio of the Minuet which follows, with its pathetic inflections and its harmonic retardations at the cadences. The Andante grazioso reminds us of Susannah's clash with Marcellina, " Io so i dover' mei . . ." and a stately introduction to the last movement, not only the most impressive movement of the Andretter music but indeed of any he has hitherto

written, reminds us of the opening of the C major
Symphony, K 338. All in all, this wedding music eclipses
the E flat Divertimento in general interest and in its
general weight. What we said about the E flat Divertimento being the best music of this period must, however, stand, for the Andretter was, after all, written in
Vienna.

# 9

## The Ninth Salzburg Period

### KEYBOARD MUSIC

*Residence :*     Flat in the Löchelplatz : house
in the Hannibalplatz
*Archbishop :*   Colloredo

THE MOZARTS RETURNED from Vienna travelling through St. Gilgen, having been much with the Mesmers in their fine house in the Landstrasse, and having made due obeisance to Salzburg's Archbishop. Their conversation included the topics of the dissolution of the Society of Jesus and the sequestration of its funds, and the Partition of Poland, proceeding happily for all but the Poles. The Mozarts rarely talked of politics. When State affairs intrude into their letters, it does in fact signify much.

Frau and Nannerl Mozart, with Miss Bimbes or Bimperl, the household dog, remained in the Löchelplatz to hear the Salzburg gossip that Wolfgang in Vienna was trying for the Kapellmeistership of the Imperial Court, Gassmann, the holder of the office, being ill. Leopold angrily contradicted this report, but no doubt would not have minded the accomplished fact.

For the first time, the son does not write on the same paper as his father. His boyish nonsense seems at last rather a strain, and as Leopold managed everything, Wolfgang felt there was nothing else to do : either scribble nonsense, or not write at all.

His father indeed was clearly in a nervous mood during this visit, and was sarcastic with his wife over not sending him a suit to wear. The death of an old friend, his doctor, Niderl, did not improve things.

As for Wolfgang, he is depicted by his father as continually at the clavier, and this picture of him may well usher in the Ninth Salzburgian Period, which saw so much of his clavier music written.

It was to a changed environment that they returned. Sometime before, the exact date is not known, the family residence had moved from the flat in the Löchelplatz to a whole house at the corner of the Hannibalplatz on the other side of the river. Nowadays it is just a bombed site opposite the Hotel Bristol, in the same square, renamed the Makartplatz after a painter belonging to a later generation. When the Mozarts were reunited in their new house after the return from Vienna in 1773 it faced the Theatre in which touring companies performed plays, including *Thamos*, for which Wolfgang had written some incidental music in the last period.

While their new house was further from the Residenz, it was nearer the Mirabell : all one can say is, that the move gave them more room without really taking them out of the Archbishop's orbit. The only person from whom they were removed was Michael Haydn at the other end of the city, but, although they disliked his wife, they had no particular motive to keep away from him.

During this period Lolli made one of his few effective entries as Kapellmeister, reducing Domenico Fischietti to the rank of a coadjutor. Leopold therefore found himself No. 3 of a hierarchy whose changes did allow him often to occupy the No. 2 place and sometimes, for a few giddy months, that of No. 1 itself. No acting captain, substantive lieutenant, took the matter more seriously.

In more purely family matters, the only event secondary to the house removal was the replacement of the late Dr. Niderl by Dr. Barisani, who was the Archbishop's doctor, too.

As for Wolfgang and music, it will be easy to see that this period is his greatest to date. For the first time in Salzburg his music is dominated by the pianoforte. Of those works which do not include this instrument it will not be necessary to deal, except for a few of more than usual interest. These are firstly a couple of symphonies, the enchanting K 201 in A and its companion, K 200 in C. Secondly a group of seven Epistle sonatas, and thirdly the opera on which he began to work at the very end of the period, *La Finta Giardiniera*, taking the MS. of it on his next journey, which was to Munich. Fourthly, and aesthetically justly last, the bassoon concerto K 191, a work included here because it is one of the best known of Mozart's output at this time. Its popularity is an example of the luck of the concert hall : some bassoon players wish to play a concerto, there is but one example by a master in the whole repertoire, and thus Mozart's K 191 is heard from time to time, while the much more enlivening and original K 225 is not heard at all. This is the chief of the six Epistle sonatas written during this period, and is an extended Allegro in A with a delightfully promising second subject which, however, finishes its eight-bar course in an adequate, but conventional manner. K 212 is noticeable for a pompously impressive development of twelve bars. K 244 and K 245 have the organ part fully written out, for manuals only, and with a harpsichord texture. K 274 of 1777, a year later, reverts to the bass line for the organ, which is not even figured. In contrast to this, a " Sonate pro festis Palii " has a carefully figured bass, and this K 278 is the first of the Epistle sonata group scored orchestrally. The two other examples of orchestral writing occur in later periods.

Now the pianoforte works in this period are :—

K 179 " Fischer " Variations
K 279 in C, a Sonata
K 280 in F, a Sonata
K 281 in B flat, a Sonata
K 282 in E flat, a Sonata
K 283 in G, a Sonata
K 312 in G minor (first movement only).

There is one concerto, that in D, K 175.

It is not known what instrument Mozart had in mind for these solo sonatas. It may have been the pianoforte, though the famous meeting with Stein, during which Mozart saw his factory and was most impressed, had not yet taken place. The argument in favour of these sonatas being for the clavichord is that this instrument had been in the Mozart household since the return from the great Paris–London tour of the composer's childhood, and that the name of C. P. E. Bach, an undoubted clavichord writer, was important to them all. Indeed, the sonatas of C. P. E. Bach were specifically mentioned as his son's model in the letter which Leopold sent to Breitkopf and Hartel from Munich, to which capital he and his son went directly after the close of this period. As for the harpsichord, that instrument was ubiquitous, though not more so in German speaking lands than the clavichord.

Internal evidence is perplexing : the sonatas sound well when played briskly and evenly, with the contrasting dynamics only of loud and soft, without any shading. They sound possibly better when played more slowly and intimately, with infinitely delicate and subtle nuances and a complete avoidance of the harpsichord's sudden dramatic change. As for the old-fashioned long or square pianoforte, they sound well enough on that, and can even be tolerated on the modern concert grand if the soloist keeps within a modest dynamic range. But if we apply the desert island test : I am to be on an island with Mozart scores of these five and a bit sonatas, and can have one instrument only : I should choose the clavichord. That is my own personal predilection, and is no argument. The clear part writing and the nature of the melodies makes me often wish to think of these works in my inner ear as a ghostly string trio in the clavichord, with perfect legato and part phrasing. But if we examine these sonatas movement by movement, it will be seen that desert island or no desert island, a clavichord will not do throughout.

K 279 consists largely, and especially in the first movement, of rather starchy material well within the competence of the harpsichord, though the last twenty-six bars of the Finale, quite orchestral in texture, need a pianoforte. The E minor—D minor section after the fermata, nineteen bars after the double bar, is of a clavichordic nature. The sfzorzando scherzo effects could be realised on a harpsichord only by a shortening

of the preceding note and a hardly-measurable pause :
the clavichord or the pianoforte can manage a sfzorzando
better.

K 280 is pianistic and dramatic, with many pianistic
figurations in the first and third movements which need
individual note accentuation to bring out the latent
melody.

The first movement of K 281 is very harpsichordic ;
take, for instance, the repeated thirds in the bass which on
a pianoforte can only with difficulty be given any crisp
brio. The second movement is, however, only harpsichordic as to the ornaments which, after all, would sound
quite well on a clavichord, which instrument could also
give full interpretative effect to the subtle dynamic levels.
As for the third movement, it would be reasonable to
decide for the harpsichord as far as bar 102, but when 103
and 105 come along, then we need the pianoforte.

K 282 in E flat is unique. It starts with a slow movement. This sonata is harpsichordic throughout, except
for a few bars starting at bar 9 after the double bar in
the last movement, which need a sustaining pedal.

K 283 has an interesting passage of fifteen bars marked
forte before the double bar of quavers grouped in pairs.
On a clavichord this can be given Bach's " tears "
anapaestic measure ; on a harpsichord the passage tends
to become emotionally null, but harmonically iridescent.
This, and the general texture of the whole sonata until
the double bar in the Finale, seems to mean the harpsichord. This Finale passage is the most arresting in the
whole rather dull work. The previous section closed with
a perfect cadence, forte, and separated by rests, in an
emphatic D major. The double bar introduces D minor
without preparation and needs an instrument capable

of holding the crotchet and making it sing with the quaver after it : a pianoforte or clavichord rather than a harpsichord, then. There follows four bars of an essentially pianistic diminished seventh arpeggio. Then the whole thing is repeated in A minor, and the arpeggios lengthen themselves to and merge into general harpsichord matter more in keeping with the remainder of the work.

The fragment in G minor, K 312, is the Allegro of an unfinished sonata. It is apart from the other six first movements, five of them Allegros and one of them the unique Andante of K 282. This G minor Allegro has thematic substance which is much stronger and more passionate than its five fellows. The actual writing, however, is sparser, as though it were merely a sketch for filling in later. Were it not reasonably well authenticated, and were the themes weaker, it might be doubted if the work was indeed by Wolfgang or, if by him, then at this time. It was rare at any time for him to write a sketch. His constant improvisations, both to himself and to his friends, must, however, often have yielded music of the greatest value, and perhaps this single movement is the jotting down, as quickly as possible, of one such improvisation. This word, in the Romantic era, connoted often enough a rambling, " poetic " piece, but we may be as sure with Mozart as with J. S. Bach, that improvisations were as formally clear and as balanced as any of their written work. Einstein, by the way [E1], dismisses the whole problem by dating the movement 1790.

If we follow Einstein, rather than the earlier Köchel or Wyzewa and St. Foix [W4], or the later Hyatt King [K3], we may sum up the six sonatas as mainly harpsichord music, but with some unaccountable passages which would not be fully effective on that instrument, and not bother about K 312.

In the variations on a minuet by Fischer, K 179, played later in the Duchesse de Chobot's ice-cold reception room in Paris, we have the pure harpsichordist, including, in the ninth variation, crossing of hands in the manner of Scarlatti. So much is this a harpsichord work, that it cannot be played on the clavichord.

But although the weight of consideration accumulates more and more towards the harpsichord, we cannot forget the clavichord in the Mozart home, that companion of the first Paris–London tour. Nor may we forget his father's remark to him in a letter from Salzburg to Paris dated 20th April 1778, that if he could find a clavichord it would suit him better (than a harpsichord) [M 18]. Although Mozart is taken as being the supreme artist in music, yet he was after all a man, and may it not be supposed that, at a time when he was comparatively inexperienced and by modern standards, still a boy, he heard his keyboard music in his mind's ear mainly on a harpsichord, but with illogical and occasional replacement by a clavichord? It was not indeed until the eighteenth century that composers made any difference in their scores whether writing for organ, virginals, clavichord or harpsichord. They were interchangeable. J. S. Bach and his sons made a distinction, and Wolfgang was beginning to do so. Anyone playing these Salzburg sonatas slowly on a pianoforte (not too slowly, of course) with a keen sense of nuance, and taking the utmost pleasure in the harmonic flow and such part writing as presents itself, will see how different they are in style from the Fischer variations, and that these sonatas,

H

Italianate and to some extent harpsichordic, yet are half-brothers to the unquestionably clavichord sonatas of C. P. E. Bach.

The sonata for four hands, in B flat, K 358, is obvious harpsichord music, and of less interest than K 381 in D, which is usually dated earlier, and with which we dealt in Chapter 7.

The concerto, K 175, was for harpsichord, being noted "Concerto per il Clavicembalo" [G4] and it has nothing to teach us about Mozart's harpsichordic style, as opposed to his way of writing for the clavichord or the pianoforte, except the polyphonic interest in the last movement, for which a set of variations was substituted some years later when the work was performed on the pianoforte. The harpsichord has always been supposed to be suited for polyphony, but this is really only the case when the counterpoint does not run to more than two voices and when the instrument is such that two manuals may be used, each with a different registration. A single manual harpsichord would be inferior to a clavichord, as allowing little difference in touch or in phrasing to distinguish two different themes played simultaneously; in which art the harpsichord is also inferior to the pianoforte.

But the main evidence for the harpsichord, apart from its title, lies in the general form of the work rather than in the moment to moment detail. It is a common observation nowadays on the part of advocates of the harpsichord that it mingles with string tone, while the pianoforte does not. It is this very mingling with the string tone which made the harpsichord concerto like the violin concerto, and which made something quite distinct of the pianoforte concerto. The Bach concerto, whether by J. S. Bach himself in his arrangements of his own or someone else's violin concerto, or by C. P. E. Bach or that concerto art of J. C. Bach which the little Wolfgang set himself to copy when in London, had a continual ripple of harpsichord tone throughout, whether by a second instrument filling in the figured bass (the vestigial remains of which lasted to Beethoven) or by the soloist never ceasing his chatter. From time to time the orchestra, in the Bach concerto, pauses, when the harpsichord is more clearly heard. Then once more the strings join in, adding to the tone and slightly submerging that of the harpsichord. The singing of the thrush overlays the ripple of the brook : when the bird ceases, the brook sounds louder, but is really rippling exactly as before. The thrush is the string tone ; the brook the harpsichord.

But, later on, when the pianoforte arrived, there came a change, because its tone is different from that of the harpsichord. Mozart began to give the soloist his own thematic material, making a personality out of the pianoforte different from and opposed to that of the orchestra, thus making a strength (a dramatic opposition) out of a weakness (the pianoforte tone and the orchestral tone being unhappy together).

The thematic material of K 175 is the same for both orchestra and soloist, and requires a really good harpsichord, or else, with a single manual instrument or one whose stops do not operate each keyboard individually, the Alberti bass is too prominent. It becomes maddeningly prominent, in fact, quite as maddening as in J. C. Bach.

That a good harpsichord was essential to a concerto is shown when, later on, Nannerl refused to play at the Lodrons because their best instrument was not available.

If we have shown that K 175 was therefore a harpsichord work and not a pianoforte one, we may return to the sonatas, as they have been mainly responsible for a certain amount of controversy regarding the aesthetic merits of Mozart's keyboard writing as a whole. As his sonatas are among the best known of all his Salzburg compositions, no apology is necessary for dwelling so much upon them here. The nineteenth-century writers either ignored Mozart as a classic upon whom Romanticism had turned its back, or deified him as an angel child who could do no wrong; in other words, romanticising him, and turning him into what he was not.

The comparison of his early sonatas with the three of Beethoven's Op. 2 has provoked a reaction which is as extreme as it is unjust. These Salzburg sonatas are not more interesting than those of Haydn upon which some writers consider they were modelled. Haydn's sonatas of his First and Second Period, using Geiringer's classification [G 8] are often trivial, but they work up to the solidity and emotional force of that in D, sometimes numbered Op. 53, No. 2, or No. 9 in the Breitkopf collection, and No. 19 in the KG enumeration, and composed in 1767, when Haydn was 34. But this comparison of the early sonatas of the two men is difficult, because of the extraordinary differences of their musical personalities. Mozart is sparer, more athletic, slyer, and less personally involved. Haydn is heavier, often more musically obvious, sometimes more emotional and, when he is so, deeply involved. The nearest equivalent of Mozart's Salzburg sonatas is to me the harpsichord music of Purcell, which has the same spareness, objectivity and pleasure in textual experiment. And Purcell's harpsichord music is deprecated by some in the same manner as Mozart's early harpsichord and clavichord work. Both bring the pianist into direct touch with the composer, both sets of works are always artistic and refined, and both remind us of appropriate vocal music.

It must be made clear that this comparison, or that with Haydn, or even that with Beethoven's Op. 2, only deals with the Salzburg works. If this book dealt with the Fantasia and Sonata in C minor, we would write very differently. " Mozart's Sonatas " are not one entity. He did not, like Haydn or Beethoven, or like Bach with the clavichord, use the form throughout his life, as Wordsworth thought Milton did with the sonnet, to express utterances otherwise unheard. Mozart never really considered the solo pianoforte sonata as of great importance though, being Mozart, he has written some scattered movements for the pianoforte which are among the very greatest penned by any composer since the introduction of that instrument. But " Mozart's Sonatas " are neither great music, nor hack work, nor juvenilia, nor anything else. They have to be split into groups before any epithets will fit.

The great symphonies challenge the title of this chapter. Perhaps, after all, it is not keyboard music which might reasonably give this period its name ?

K 183, in G minor, has an arresting first movement which is so terse and even rough that it marks a Mozartian extreme. The Minuet is impressive, and the Finale full of prophecies. There is no Salzburgian equivalent to this symphony which, had it never been found owing to some MS. destruction or other, could not have been guessed at. Now such works as the E flat piano concerto could be guessed if we knew the work for two pianos and the Sinfonia Concertante.

K 200 in C major is the second of these three symphonies : it is much more Salzburgian, and has its parallels in several sonata movements.

K 201 in A is also typical. The delightful theme of the first movement and the charming subject in the dominant which follows, gives us two Mozartian graces easy to recognise : one is the making of a melody from a cadence (in this case marking the dominant to bring in the codetta before the double bar) and the other is to introduce a sequential passage of striking individuality into the working-out. Above all, Mozart shows in each of these symphonies his special gift for endless surprise : when all seems to have been said, there is still something further, and even more miraculous, to add.

The bassoon concerto is interesting only because it is for that instrument ; otherwise it is an empty work, with very little of the symphonic about it, only just enough ritornelli to justify the presence of an orchestra, and plenty of bassoon passage-work.

In books on early Mozart much is made of the galant, a fashionable something which means facile melody and simple accompaniment, and which does not mean the sombre, the tragic or the polyphonic. But to me very little of Mozart's music of any period is galant, even when he may have supposed himself to be writing in this way. What is facile melody ? Mozart's was usually easy to come by—to Mozart. That which can be developed, that which is developed and that which is episodal or contrasting, these are the Mozartian melodies. He rarely uses an isolated melody for its own sake, and while a Handel or a Schubert melody may often be used with effect out of its context, few Mozart melodies mean quite so much if taken out of the work of which they form an integral part. This does not mean, it is hardly necessary to say, any superiority on the part of any one of these great men : it is merely a different way of working. Mozart and Handel have, by the way, one thing in common, which is " composing." The power and beauty of their work often lies to some extent in the arrangement of material, some of which may be commonplace. Those long sections in Handel and those shorter sections in Mozart which, taken bodily out of the work and printed in a textbook, could fairly be called, conventional, humdrum, hack work, and so on, are not always the result of writing too much. As in the famous section before the repeat in Mozart's " great " E flat symphony, first movement, and as in almost any Handel organ concerto, the slabs of concrete are there for structural purposes. Both composers " architect " their works, using this, using that, sometimes deliberately using something dull to offset something miraculous. All this is largely by the way : but we only have to think how different are, let us say, Chopin or Wagner, whose every bar is expected to bear the stamp of genius.

To return to Salzburg. We must deal, though briefly, with the opera *La Finta Giardiniera*, which was begun before the departure for Munich late in 1774. This was a three-act opera buffa of a total of twenty-eight numbers, the same length in this respect as *Figaro* was to be. It is strange to think that a Mozart opera written after such glowing works as the A major symphony, K 201, the witty Andretter music with its prophetic *Figaro* passages and the brilliant Milanese *Exsultate*, *Jubilate* should not be in any regular repertoire : only Sandrina's aria in the first Act, *Noi donne poverine*, is at all known. Although this work partly existed in MS. before

Mozart took it, incomplete, to Munich, its examination is really outside the scope of this book. It would appear, indeed, out of the scope of most books : even Professor Dent gives it a mere page, and it is to Wyzewa and Saint-Foix that we owe by far the longest examination, of more than eight pages. It is, however, an extra-Salzburg work, being written to the commission of the Elector of Bavaria, and performed in Munich.

Of course this aroused some interest in Salzburg society, and Frau von Robinig, of the beautiful house in the outskirts of Salzburg in which the traditional Austrian-Alpine style is enriched by the baroque, took Nannerl with her daughter Louise to Munich to hear it. Mozart's operatic star continued to wax : he had been commissioned by Maria Theresa herself for Milan, had just gone to Munich for an Electoral command, and now even his own country acknowledged the prophet.

The Archbishop would have had opportunities of hearing Mozart in opera, apart from the stiff *Il Sogno di Scipione*. Colloredo was in the habit of inviting visiting troupes to perform in the Residenz, and thus would have heard arias which Wolfgang wrote for such visitors in the autumn of 1775—K 217, for instance, *Voi Avete un cor fedele*, written to help the production of an opera by Galuppi one of whose male parts had had to be cut. Thus an aria of Dorina the maidservant addressed to two lovers had to be altered to Dorina addressing herself to the task of dismissing only one. In the strains of Susanna rather than of Despina she sets about the task in music which, in its several felicitous touches, is mature Mozart.

Thus when the Chief Steward of the Archiepiscopal Court began to consider how best to welcome Maria

Theresa's youngest son, the Archduke Maximilian, when he paid his intended visit to Salzburg, he thought of Mozart, and the Archbishop agreed that the young man could do very well.

And so to the Tenth Period, and *Il Re Pastore*.

# 10

# The Tenth Salzburg Period

## BEFORE PARIS

*Residence :*    House in the Hannibalplatz
*Archbishop :*   Colloredo.

THE RETURN FROM Munich and *La Finta Giardiniera* was on 7th March 1775, and immediately Wolfgang plunged into the composition of *Il Re Pastore*. This haste was because no one had troubled to communicate the Archbishop's desire for him to undertake an opera for the entertainment of Maria Theresa's youngest son, the Archduke Maximilian, while he was in Munich. By the time the Mozarts arrived home, the Archduke was himself in Munich, with Salzburg next on his itinerary. Wolfgang, always a quick worker, found most of March and some of April sufficient to finish the work. On a libretto by Metastasio, it has so little action, especially in Act 2, that it reminds us of a Handel serenata, *Acis and Galatea*, for instance, rather than the bustling or dramatic plot which Wolfgang often seemed to prefer.

*Così fan Tutte*, which in its own trivial way is full of action, seems to throw its shadow of vivacity to come over the Overture in C to *Il Re Pastore*. To this brisk Allegro Mozart later added an Andante, taking Aminta's first aria for its subject, and adding a Rondo Finale to make a three-movement symphony of the whole.

St. Foix [S1] suggests that a March in C, K 214, written at this time, was intended to precede this symphony as a marching on movement, to make a serenade of the whole. No one has, however, thought it worth while publishing either symphony or serenade as a separate score ; the work is only accessible in the *Mozartgesselschaft*. The three movements were performed as a symphony at a concert in Mannheim under Cannabish.

This showed that instrumental music was in Wolfgang's mind in the spring of 1775, and another link between *Il Re Pastore* and instrumental music is to be found in Aminta's second aria in B flat.

This would electrify any listener to an unlikely revival of *Il Re Pastore* by beginning, a minor third higher but with otherwise the same harmony and orchestration of strings, oboes and horns, as the violin concerto, K 216. After this fiery introduction, however, with its forte and piano placed exactly as in the concerto, other matter supervenes, and the four bars appear only once thereafter. When Aminta begins to sing " Aer tranquillo e di sereni freschi fonti a verdi prati," she voices a sentiment which K 216 has taught us to regard as surprising in this musical context.

In this Violin Concerto in G, written in this period but after the performance of *Il Re Pastore*, the vigorous musical phrase of Aminta's aria occurs only thrice, in the orchestral exposition, in the solo exposition, and in the recapitulation. It avoids both the development and the coda, nor is it ever treated in sequence. The phrase seems to have been alive for months in its creator's brain, without engendering any linked set of paragraphs.

When the soloist takes it up from the orchestra, there is a slight melodic alteration, but the rhythm is unaltered. In the recapitulation Mozart omitted the forte and piano marks, which merely shows how much he took for granted in his scores.

*Il Re Pastore* was duly given before the Archduke and the Archbishop with Consoli the castrato from Munich as primo uomo and Mozart remembered his opera with enough affection to write out three years later for the woman (Aloysia Weber) he loved but did not marry, the four principal arias of Aminta, including the *Aer tranquillo*.

For the next two and a half years (spring 1775–autumn 1777) Wolfgang led a bustling Salzburg existence. In the great world outside the charmed Archdiocese the Partition of Poland was causing much bad temper among the three thieves. But the Mozarts were in no way disturbed.

Wolfgang composed for wealthy Salzburgians, for friends and his sister. Thun and Lodron were among the twenty best families [G1], but this information has mainly negative importance. It means that the other eighteen " best " families did not employ Mozart. The Haffners and the Lutzows are not in the list of the twenty though they were wealthy and influential. So we may suppose the Mozarts could be named as being surrounded by friendly, musical, appreciative and wealthy families such as the Thuns, Lodrons, Robinigs, Haffners, Lutzows and Andretters, provided that we remember that there were very many more families who either had never heard of Wolfgang Mozart, or who were indifferent, or even hostile to him. It was really a clique life, in which intrigue played its due part. This suited Leopold

Mozart, for he understood intrigue, or thought he did. But his son was very different, and though friendly and approachable, yearned for the larger musical sphere of a great city.

*Friends*

An alphabetical list of friends is given in a letter from Wolfgang when in Mannheim on his journey to Paris at the end of this period. It was written in obvious high spirits, and its accuracy no doubt suffers accordingly. This happiness was due to the influence of travel on a mercurial temperament and perhaps he had already met Aloysia Weber : his unhappiness in Salzburg is depicted in a portrait painted during this period by an unknown artist. It shows a man older than his twenty years, who looks quite ill. But Mannheim certainly set him up.

Adlgasser, Cathedral organist.

Andretter, the family for whom he wrote the wedding music already described.

Arco, the Court Chamberlain, his wife and their household, including their chambermaid nicknamed " Sallerl."

Bullinger, the Abbé : confessor to the Arcos.

Barisani (the error in alphabetical arrangement is Wolfgang's) the new doctor to the Mozarts who was also private physician to the Archbishop.

Berantsky, of whom nothing is known.

Czernin, Count, nephew of the Archbishop and brother of Countess Lutzow, wife of the fortress commander. Count Czernin was a keen amateur violinist and conductor. He had a red face and stuttered when excited.

Cusetti, a Court violinist.

Daser, a tailor who made for the Mozarts.

Deibl, flute and oboe player in the Court orchestra : he was one of those friends for whom Wolfgang cried when he was 7 and away from home.

Eberlin, Barbara, daughter of the famous Eberlin who had been one of the most talented of the Kapell-meisters.

Gilowsky family, the daughter of which, " Katherl," ranked in the Mozarts' affections with " Sallerl " (maid of the Arcos). The father of the household was a doctor, and later, in Vienna, acted as Wolf-gang's best man at his wedding with Constanza.

Goschwendner, Franz Xaver, ironmonger in Getreide-gasse. His brother worked in Korman's Bank in Paris and acted for Wolfgang on the forthcoming Paris journey.

Haydn, Michael, organist and conductor from the key-board of the Court orchestra when the Konzert-meister was not present to lead from the first violins. He married Maria Magdalena Lipp, daughter of the Cathedral's second organist.

Hagenauer, the Mozarts' landlord in their Löchelplatz days.

Joli, Rosalie. Nicknamed " Sallerl," see under Arco.

Janitsch, Anton. Violinist from the orchestra of a local dignitary near Augsburg. Janitsch's playing was much admired by Leopold Mozart.

Kuhnburg, Count and Countess. A Salzburg Court official and his wife. When Wolfgang was 6 he met the then unmarried but already affianced Countess Kuhnburg in Vienna. The families con-tinued their friendship. A governess to the Kuhn-burg children took violin lessons from Nannerl and played Wolfgang's music. The Kuhnburgs were anxious about Wolfgang's moral welfare when he was in Paris.

Lutzow, Countess. Wife of the Citadel Commander and a niece of the Archbishop's. Wolfgang wrote K 246 for her. Her uncle thought she influenced Mozart in the wrong direction.

Lodron, Count and Countess. Army Commander of the Salzburg area. The Countess was a patron and friend of the Mozarts. Wolfgang wrote several works for her and her family, including the concerto for three harpsichords for the Countess and her two daughters. They had one son. Leopold Mozart called Count Lodron " Count Potbelly."

Joseph Meisner, a bass singer. He also taught. Like the Mozarts, he was out of Salzburg often enough and for long enough at a time to make the Archbishop testy, and he was reprimanded also for pleading excuses for not singing in the Cathedral when he was in residence. He was of Leopold's generation and his voice did not wear well. Probably his excuses were sometimes genuine. In spite of some criticism, Wolfgang had a genuine regard for Meisner as a singer.

Frau von Robinig and her family. Unlike most of Mozart's other patrons, this wealthy family aspired no higher than the " von," the lowest rank of nobility. They owned a town house as well as a country farm a few kilometres outside Salzburg. This country residence was built in the traditional manner, with large expanse of roof with one roof line and a single huge gable at each end, and with numerous rococo excrescences added. The Robinigs' money came from property in mines.

Rust, Jacob. " Maestro " Rust : by the time Wolfgang
reached the letter R in his alphabet of friends, he
was tiring of seriously thinking (if he had indeed
started with this intention): he now begins to pun,
to include enemies and so forth. Rust was never
a particular friend of the Mozarts. He became
Kapellmeister in 1777 with Fischietti. Rust was the
senior of the two men, and his appointment got in
the way of Leopold Mozart's hopes.

Theresa (" Treserl "), the Mozarts' maid in their Hannibalplatz house.

Zezi, name of a grocer in the Getreidegasse. Barbara
Zezi was a pupil of Nannerl.


We find ourselves irresistibly, even if irrelevantly,
reminded of Pepys who, equally with Wolfgang Mozart,
had friends drawn from all ranks of society. In the lives
of both men the same names recur again and again. The
personages who bore them required much handling,
and some of them sometimes got quite out of hand.
Pepys was also similar to Wolfgang in his general friendliness and approachability. Even their one great point of
difference shows their characters in the light of the same
social circumstances. While Pepys really did admire the
Earl of Sandwich and was made personally happy as
well as financially comfortable by his regard, Wolfgang
felt a personal indifference which later amounted to
hostility to the Archbishop. Even at the beginning,
words and attentions from Colloredo left him unmoved,
for he wanted work to do, work suited to his powers.

Omitted from the list of the Mozarts' friends are—
Joseph Leutgeb, a horn player. He had recently left
Salzburg to set up a shop dealing in dairy produce,

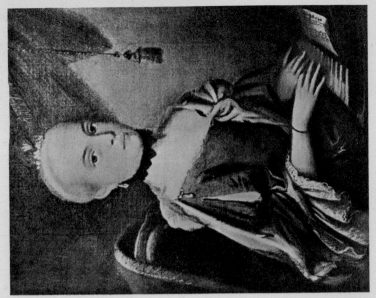

5b Louise von Robinig

5a Colloredo

6b Constanza

6a Aloysia widowed

especially cheese, in Vienna. He continued to play the
horn, and as he had been particularly intimate with
Leopold Mozart with whom he had shared part of the
Milanese sojourn in which Leopold had shammed
rheumatism, the distance did not quench their friendship.
Wolfgang was to write four horn concertos for him :
perhaps he did not value Leutgeb as much as did Leopold,
and Einstein [E1] will have it that Wolfgang laughed at
Leutgeb, or at least, at his instrument. While he may
have amused himself with those limitations of the horn
which he later on knew so well to turn to account, no
hearer of such passages as bars 16 onwards in the first
movement of the E flat horn quintet, K 407, written for
Leutgeb, could suppose that Wolfgang was laughing all
the time. To laugh some of the time, even in serious sur-
roundings was, of course, very much his way, and as for
the person of Herr Leutgeb, when in spirits Wolfgang
would mock anyone, from the Mufti downwards, except
his parents and Joseph Haydn.

Joseph Hulber of Krumbach in Swabia. This violinist
and flautist entered the Salzburg Court orchestra in
1749 [D1] and his son entered a monastery.

Anton Stadler, the clarinettist, was particularly close to
Mozart in later Vienna days and enjoys immortality for
his " creating " the Clarinet Quintet.

Joseph Fiala, an oboe player, left Salzburg for Mannheim, in which capital he witnessed the increasing influence of Mozart's music in that important symphonic
centre.

## Music and Patronage

Some of the friends just listed were among those who
commissioned music from Wolfgang Mozart.

I

1. For Countess Lodron and her two daughters, a concerto for three harpsichords and orchestra. This work also exists in an alternative form, made by the composer, for two harpsichords and orchestra. K 242.

2. For Countess Lutzow, a solo pianoforte concerto in C, K 246.

3. For Countess Lodron, a Divertimento in B flat, K 287. It was played several times at the Lodrons in the winter of 1775–6, sometimes by an amateur orchestra which met there for practice, and the Divertimento was always greeted with applause. In July 1778 this Divertimento and the one with the Köchel number 247 were played in the street outside the Andretters' house.

4. A third work for Countess Lodron was a Divertimento in F for horn and strings, K 247, with a March with its own Köchel number of 248. This work and K 287 mentioned above were both played in the street outside the Andretters' house in July 1778.

5. For Countess Lutzow, a solo pianoforte concerto in C, K 246.

6. When Count von Spaur was consecrated Priest by the Archbishop in the Cathedral, a Mass, K 258, was written for this consecration. Belonging to a noble family, von Spaur inevitably rose in the hierarchy, and became Dean of the Cathedral.

7. For his sister's twenty-first birthday, Wolfgang wrote the Divertimento in D, K 251.

8. For the daughter of the late Sigmund Haffner, Elizabeth, on her marriage to a M. Spath, a Serenade in D, K 250. This is the most famous of Mozart's wedding compositions (excluding his own personal marriage music, the great unfinished C minor Mass), and is indeed listed by St. Foix among the symphonies. Like K 247

and K 287 written for the Countess Lodron and played in the street later, this Serenade for the Haffners was also used as summer open air music.

9. For the Archbishop himself, several works: K 213 in F, K 240 in B flat, K 289 in E flat, K 270 in B flat, K 289 in E flat, and perhaps K 252 in E flat. All these works were short and slight, for oboes, horns and bassoons, and were to be played during the Archbishop's repasts in the Mirabell. Leopold Mozart later complained that his son had not been paid anything for this Table music.

10. Again for the Archbishop, but this time for his solemn Residential dinners where, in common with the King of Denmark, he shared the custom of Elsinore,

> And, as he drains his draughts of Rhenish down,
> The kettle drum and trumpet thus bray out
> The triumph of his pledge.

Thus for trumpets and drums, six of one and four of the other with the addition of two flutes, are K 187 in F and K 188 in C, each Köchel number containing a set of six fanfares.

11. Perhaps for the two young ladies of the Lodron family, or perhaps for the evening of Nannerl's twenty-fifth birthday, the Serenata notturna in D, K 239.

12. A scena and aria, " Ah, lo previdi," K 272, written for the Bohemian singer Josepha Duschek on a visit she paid to Salzburg. This was Wolfgang's first meeting with a lady who afterwards, with her husband in Prague, gave him help and hospitality.

Besides these eleven works known to be for employers, friends and relations, there are three works whose commission or other origin is unknown.

Divertimento in B flat, K 254, is a title which rather more disguises a modern chamber music form than did Divertimento in D, K 136. For this later work is a real trio for pianoforte, violin and 'cello, whereas the earlier work was only a string quartet in its slow movement, the outer movements, especially the first, being imagined as for string orchestra, with the drumming bass and reiterated notes so tedious in chamber music. In the B flat trio again the slow movement is more conversational with the interest reasonably well spread among the three talkers. If in the score the pianist seems to have the most interesting time, in performance it is the violin which tends to dominate. For when pianoforte competes with violin in scale passages and in melodic outlines, perhaps indeed competing in unison, it is the violin which dominates.

Serenade in D, a summer work, K 204.

Notturno in D, K 286.

For himself Mozart wrote concertos. Seven of these may be classified as important works, and only one (K 271) was for someone else to play.

Violin concerto in G, K 216.

Violin concerto in D, K 218.

Violin concerto in A, K 219.

Adagio for violin and orchestra in E, K 261.

Pianoforte concerto in B flat, K 238.

Pianoforte concerto in C, K 246.

Pianoforte concerto in E flat, K 271.

There was also some Church music.

This very productive period shows Mozart working usually as a sort of musical architect. He built, or composed, this or that musical edifice for his clients. Only in some of his concertos and in one or two other places was he working as an unfettered musical artist. We should not therefore expect more from this output than it is likely to yield.

We might now perhaps survey some of these works, not by patron, but by designation. To begin with the open air, occasional and general society orchestral music.

*Society Music*

Most editions of the score of the Divertimento in B flat for two horns and strings, K 287, omit the opening and closing marches. Lovers of the later horn quintet will be disappointed in K 287 and in K 247 as well, with which work we will deal in a moment. The horns in K 287 have holding notes, or mark the rhythm, while the violins carry most of the melodic matter. There are two Minuets, of which the first alone is of distinction and delight, being on the same plane as the " horn " Minuet of 1772 in K 131. It would appear that the horn players available for the Countess Lodron's entertainment were inferior to those available for whichever entertainment Mozart wrote K 131.

The Divertimento for horns and strings in F, K 247, also written for the Countess Lodron, is quite as disappointing as K 287, and for the same reason : the horns have very little else but harmonic padding and coloration. In one of the most delightful passages, that in B flat in the last movement when the first violins play high above an empty bustle with detached bass notes, the horns are indeed quite silent, but in the equally charming second Minuet they have rhythmic as well as harmonic work to do. This Divertimento is also fitted with a March, K 248, and one of infectious levity it is.

Of all the Serenades, the one called " Haffner " is the best known. The Rondo, indeed, is as near a hackneyed work as any orchestral item in the whole repertoire, and may be heard in modern restaurants. It is tuneful, easy to follow, and makes its few points obviously. It is also long, and the dullest can recognise the chief tune before its end. The interpolated violin concerto, however, in this " Haffner " Serenade, K 250 in D, is as disappointing as that in the Andretter music. In Mozart's hands the genre was best when isolated.

The Minuets of the " Haffner " Serenade are memorable. That in G minor and the Trio of the other in D both speak of mystery : in a light *fête galante* manner, but of mystery nevertheless. The orchestration of most of the Serenade is richer than in many similar works, indeed only the absence of drums stops it from being scored like a symphony. The violin concertos with which the interpolated movements have just been unfavourably compared were indeed less richly scored.

If we may sum up the " Haffner " Serenade, K 250 ; it may be because there is so much of it, and because some of it is heard so often, that it seems a specimen of galant music merely. Only here and there seems it irradiated by its composer's genius, to which it does a disservice, allowing the semi-musical to carry away from a performance of this Serenade the idea that Mozart is repetitive and obvious, so that one may always tell eight bars ahead what he will do next. The Haffner marriage was, if music tells us anything, a longer and more formal affair than the jolly Andretter feast. But, and it must always be borne in mind, the composer intended neither work to be listened to phrase by phrase, score in hand, as some of us do nowadays in a concert hall or before the ampli-

fier. We bear too heavily on the light music, not only of
Mozart, but of Haydn, Handel and of J. S. Bach himself.
This music was written to please during a clatter : it is
unreasonable to take exception to the emptiness of a
Haydn Divertimento, the heavy cadences of something
Handel wrote for the Duke of Chandos or the sewing-
machine rhythms of a Brandenburg concerto movement.
But each of them was apt to be inspired in the most
unexpected places, as Brahms found in a Feldpartita,
and that is why these eighteenth-century forms have an
enduring fascination for us.

The next Köchel number, K 251, is a smaller, quicker
and on the whole gayer work than K 250. It is the
Divertimento for Nannerl's twenty-fifth birthday, on
30th July. It is introduced and terminated by marches :
the opening march is quick and lively, with a bold theme
which is merely an ornamentation of a scale passage, but
in the hands of Mozart it becomes compelling. The most
charming and suitable movement (suitable for Nannerl)
is an Andantino with a " delicious " tune. There is a
very quick Rondo which degenerates into street melody,
among, one dares to add, much rumbustious fun from
the inhabitants of the house in the Hannibalplatz.

Of all this friend and patron-serving period, the Table
music ranks about lowest in aesthetic interest, but K 270
merits a brief description. It is typical of the Mirabell
during-supper entertainment, and can be distinguished
from the more formal between-courses music of the
Residenz. In K 270, which is scored for two oboes, two
horns and two bassoons, the first and last movements are
by far the nimblest ; as early as the fourth bar it is clearly
shown that the horns can make their rhythmic interposi-
tions at crucial moments. The Andantino has the sort

of catching tune that Mozart could always turn out at command, and which reached its apotheosis in the as yet unwritten *Les Petits Riens*, composed for the Paris ballet under Noverre during the journey which terminates this Tenth Period.

K 239, a serenata notturna, could be described as for a chamber music combination concerted with orchestral strings and drums. This would not be quite accurate, for a double bass plays in the solo section instead of a 'cello. Except for some opportunities for effective phrasing, K 239 does not justify the expectations aroused by its unusual instrumentation.

K 286, a work for four orchestras, remains to be mentioned. Each orchestra consists of strings and horns, and the whole score uses naïve echo effects even more relentlessly than Purcell at his most determined. There is some evidence that this work, a serenata notturna, was written for New Year's Day 1777. Einstein [E1], admitting the summer nature of the music, explains that Mozart was fond of summoning a musical summer to warm the winter. Certainly this music would be most enjoyable if, in the open air dusk of a summer's evening, the four orchestras were arranged in four several grottos, and made their echo effects over Augustan lawns, conjuring for us the Augustan age of our own poets. But though the idea is delightful, must it be confessed that the music is no more than polished? Michael Haydn could have done as well.

This brief summary of the contents of the more interesting of the Divertimenti and Serenades will serve to show Mozart writing at pace, though always with skill and finish, what he supposed to be ephemeral music for people he knew.

The concertos, both pianoforte and violin, were more formal affairs, and show his genius to greater advantage.

## Piano Concertos

Chief among them is certainly that for pianoforte in E flat, K 271. Most of his works in this genre were for himself, but not this one. It was a visiting French pianist, Mademoiselle Lejeunehomme, for whom he wrote it. She was really a claveciniste, and though the work is usually numbered among the pianoforte concertos, it is more suited to the harpsichord than any of those written later.

The first and last movements of K 271 have a spaciousness absent from the longest of the Divertimento movements (there is nothing longer in mere length than some of the Haffner movements), and the last movement has a Minuet incorporated into it, a formal arrangement typical of this period of Mozart's life. It is, however, the slow movement in C minor which arrests us. It is the first great Mozart : the first tragic Mozart. Just as K 131 of 1772 introduces the first emotion and the first delight of a new genius, K 271 of January 1777 introduces us to that quality of his genius which ranks him with the greatest of composers : we write here only of his Salzburg music, other Köchel numbers might be advanced as both the initiating and culminating points if we considered works written in Italy or in Vienna.

The low tessitura of the string opening of the slow movement of K 271, the quasi recitativo of the soloist's first remarks, the hesitant E flat tune and later the further recitativo until we come to the full and passionate passage following letter D : these things speak as strongly of this new personal and tragic quality as does the originality of the cadenza which exploits the tone qualities of both the highest octave open to pianofortes of that time and of the " Great " octave which, though readily accessible, was not often used for thematic material in purely pianoforte work like this.[1]

There are lesser pianoforte concertos written during this period : B flat, K 238 and C, K 246. They are of more historical interest than musical and show, by the MSS. now in the Mozarteum, that the soloist filled in a quiet figured bass during the tuttis $G^4$. Beethoven too figured his basses in his first two concertos.

K 242 in F, the concerto for three harpsichords for the Lodron family, is only a little more interesting than the B flat and C major concertos just referred to. If any display of learned counterpoint is hoped for by a listener who sees three harpsichords and thinks of J. S. Bach, he will be disappointed. One of the keyboards has a very simple part written for it and Mozart himself rearranged the whole work for just two keyboards. But if hope reawakens thinking of Mozart's glorious work in E flat for two keyboards and orchestra, there will again be disappointment. Except for a good deal of demi-semiquaver ornamentation admirably suited to the harpsichord in the Adagio, there is nothing to comment upon, least of all in the dull Minuet Rondo of the Finale.

*Violin Concertos*

The three violin concertos K 216, 8 and 9 are unique. They are different in quality from Mozart's other music in this form, whether violin concerto, violin and orchestra single movement or interpolated violin and orchestral

---

[1] J. S. Bach is not in evidence although his bass fugal lines were often placed within this octave, as whatever he wrote for, he certainly did not write for pianoforte.

movement into a Divertimento. Yet they are equally different from other concertos of other composers, whether of the Italian model or prophetic of Beethoven. They are also completely different from Mozart's pianoforte concertos, except that sometimes a Rondo of one may remind us, either in its formal three-in-a-bar start, or upon meeting a sudden Minuet movement, of a Rondo of the other. But this similarity is a paper one : there is no similarity of musical feeling except once, and then strangely. For it is not Mozart at all, but the last movement of a concerto for harpsichord and orchestra in D by Haydn which has considerable " gipsy " resemblance to the brilliant finale of K 219.

In these three concertos, Mozart's way of writing for the violin is characteristic. It is not insipid, as in even the concerto movements of the Haffner K 250, it is not occupied with themes suitable for contrapuntal development as in J. S. Bach, nor has it anything in common with the technically difficult double stopping common in concertos after Paganini. Mozart's characteristics in the solo violin writing in these concertos lie in the contrast between tone in the violin's high and low registers, in the effects to be produced by cantilena, and in a texture which allows of modulations brought about by melodic rather than by directly harmonic means, and in chromatic melody, especially the interval of a semitone. An example of this is in the G major second entry of the soloist in the first movement of K 216 at bar 51, when the flowing chromatic melody, though throughout in the tonic, hints at A major and E minor. It is this chromaticism which tends to shift the key, and this is perhaps the secret of the " speaking " utterances which Mozart wrings from the soloist.

But was not Mozart influenced at all in these violin concertos of which we write ? Boccherini and Geminiani are named, among others, and while it does indeed seem that there is a certain similarity between Boccherini (i.e., the Amoroso movement of Op. 13, No. 5) and the Salzburg Mozart, this relationship is not found most fully displayed in these concertos. In the very different work for three harpsichords for instance, the figuration might be derived from violin ornamentation of Italian composers. But, except for one thing, the differences between K 216, 8 and 9 on the one hand and all the violin concertos of all other composers on the other, are much greater than the similarities. And the single exception refers to Haydn, as we have already mentioned.

In the series of Köchel numbers which constitute the violin concertos just under discussion, it will have been noticed that one number, K 217, was missing. This is not a violin work at all, but an aria.

To K 219 there is alternative slow movement to be found in K 261, simpler but almost equally sensitive and passionate. Gaetano Brunetti, first violin and soloist in the Court orchestra at Salzburg (M 19) was the onlie begetter, as he was also of K 269, a Rondo for violin and orchestra in B flat.

This admits of a little speculation. Wolfgang Mozart himself was of course Konzertmeister, but when journeying he was not paid. So it may be that though W. A. Mozart had the title, Brunetti very often did the work, especially when the Vice-Kapellmeister, that Adjutant of the music, was himself away in company of the Konzertmeister. Yet it created the sort of situation about which the Vice-Kapellmeister himself thought it reasonable to complain, that, for instance, his son was not paid when not on duty. Brunetti, too, had his grievance : he in fact led the orchestra, but without either the honour or pay of a Konzertmeister. That Mozart wrote several concertos for the violin and we may suppose played them himself is our gain : that he wrote two separate movements for Brunetti showed his good nature as well.

We have some letters the Mozart family wrote from Salzburg during this period. Disappointingly, they do not, however, refer to a visit which the Emperor paid to Salzburg as he travelled from Vienna to Paris to see his sister, the Queen, and to sound his pretended ally Louis XVI on the subjects of the Hanoverian succession and the Partition of Poland. He was not markedly successful, the French not caring in the least that the Emperor feared that very Russian incursion into Europe which the Partition itself invited, and noted with amusement Joseph's attempts to hide predatory feelings towards Bavaria.

In Salzburg, the Emperor visited the Residenz and inspected the main apartments, saying good-bye in the Carabinier Room, and then resumed his seat in his coach. Except that every Salzburgian eye was on every detail of the visit, and a Field Marshal brother of the Archbishop's was invited to add military glamour to the proceedings, there was nothing to mark this adventure of a day from other days, for officially it was but the visit of a Graf von Falkenstein [W1]. Had the Emperor visited Salzburg officially, and not incognito, then indeed both the Mozarts would have been deeply involved, composing and rehearsing special music for the occasion.

Among the letters is one which Leopold Mozart

wrote to Breitkopf, the music publisher of Leipzig, to ask if he would print some of his son's scores. It was a typical Leopoldian letter, clear, sensible, but a little acrid, with the amateur in business's hint that there were other firms as well as Breitkopf's in the world. It also asked three questions, one at the end of the letter, and two lumped together in a postscript. This method of letter-writing was used in much of his correspondence, a going on and on, a mannerism which much annoyed his son later and which was partly the cause of the rupture.

Far different is Wolfgang's letter to Padre Maestro Martini of Bologna. Its general lines were much as might be expected from the son of Leopold : moral sentiments and grumbles and the desire to retain a profitable and influential friend. But Wolfgang the alive, the quick-minded and the disinterested, is present in all the many asides : no castrati at the moment in Salzburg because they demand such fees, praise of Michael Haydn and of Adlgasser, the information that a whole Mass, from Kyrie to Agnus Dei, must not last more than three-quarters of an hour less a few minutes to be dedicated to the Epistle sonata. With this letter he sent to Padre Martini a Latin work written on his return to Salzburg before this period opened. It was avowedly based on a certain work by Eberlin, whose Latin music, with that of Michael Haydn, he had copied before and was to copy again. It transpired, six years or so later, that he considered Eberlin and his own exercises in Eberlin's manner sufficiently similar to the style of Handel to make this sort of music acceptable in the van Swieten circle in Vienna.

When there was no work to be done, the Mozarts and their friends would spend a good deal of time shooting darts out of air guns. This undignified sport was very popular with Vice-Kapellmeister, Konzertmeister, the Abbé Bullinger and other officials on Sunday afternoons. Girls often joined them, Nannerl and her friends, including the chambermaid of the Arcos. The targets were hand-drawn depictions of family life, jokes at love affairs, teasing and " robust " at times, and often adorned with little verses. There would be betting as to who hit the target first.

Wolfgang was exceedingly attractive to some women, and his numerous flirtations might have resulted in early marriage to some suitable girl had it not been for his tragedy, which was to love an ambitious and capable singer whom he was fated to meet in Mannheim on that journey to Paris which closes this period. But at the moment he is still heart whole, and it would appear that the daughter of the Court Baker found it necessary to enter a convent because of unrequited passion. This seems amusing to us, and it was so a little later both to Leopold and Wolfgang : it could have been hardly so delightful for the poor girl. Wolfgang's views on marriage and on chastity are clear. He wrote later that his temperament needed marriage, he wished to marry, and found it difficult to remain chaste. Yet he pursued none of the attractive girls who seemed to beckon him, and after his meeting with Aloysia Weber, the pain this hard woman caused him diminished his interest in women until the time came when he was content to marry Aloysia's sister : " the Weber in the blood." But, alas for the baker's daughter.

As for Wolfgang's life among his MSS., his friends and his ideas, we know that he was becoming untidy and, apart from music, always remained so. He disliked

walking. The family shooting games were more to his
taste. But above all he grew more and more restless for
the great world outside, a restlessness which was irri-
tated from time to time by the knowledge of various
friends securing appointments elsewhere. He was shut
in by the mountains which skirted the smiling Salzach
valley with its central heights of the Festung and the
Kapusinerberg.

On 1st August 1777, he wrote to Colloredo, with the
obvious help of his father. It was rather a trying letter,
which seemed to lecture the Archbishop on morality.
No doubt Archbishops need such lectures, but Colloredo
was not the man to relish them. A homily to the bachelor
on the duties of parents and to the priest on the parable
of the talents were altogether too much : the Archbishop
kept the letter for four weeks without doing anything,
and then minuted to the Court Chamberlain (Arco), a
cold " father and son have my permission to find work
elsewhere." This on the face of it meant no more pay
for either, and had Leopold known of this minute,
which he may have done either through the Abbé or
through Sallerl, he would have regretted his part in the
compilation of the homily. But the times were propitious
for him, Kapellmeister Lolli was too ill to perform his
duties, and the competence and experience of Leopold
made him a valuable musical administrator, possessing
qualities absent in Fischietti (the nominal senior Kapellmeister) and the newly imported Rust. Further, Colloredo
did not seem, at this time at any rate, to bear grudges. He
forbore or forgot to issue the necessary orders for
cancellation of pay to his pay office, and later sent a
vague letter of goodwill which did, however, make one
thing quite clear, that Leopold Mozart might still regard

7b Schrattenbach

7a Cardinal Thun's triumph

8a The Mozart family

8b Salzburg in Schubert's time

himself as Vice-Kapellmeister. This suited Leopold, for although he had great ambitions for his son, his own purpose was to cling to the Salzburg salary until he certainly and without doubt found something better.

So started a time of strain in the household of the Hannibalplatz. Where should Wolfgang go? Who should go with him? May he not go alone? No, at least to the last. As for Leopold going away, he had obviously overplayed his hand with the Archbishop, and his very great sense of caution counselled him not to be too prominent in any way for a while. He must stay behind in Salzburg and mind himself. Frau Mozart loved society just as much as her son did. If she herself went with Wolfgang, she would lose her many friends for a while. If they went as far away as Paris, then she might be away from Salzburg for more than a year. From the dignified circle of Frau von Molk, Frau von Gerlichs, Frau Hagenauer and Fraulein Maria Raab (their new landlord) down to the girls, Sallerl, Katherl and little Victoria Adlgasser, daughter of the Cathedral organist, who attended on Nannerl to do her hair, Frau Mozart found there was much to leave. Born into the minor nobility, Frau Mozart had a different view of life from her saving, intriguing self-made husband. She could more easily assume that her circumstances of tolerable, if just tolerable, ease were always to be hers as a sort of right, and did not demand constant effort on her part to maintain them.

As for Leopold, he was strong for Paris. A post in a minor Court near Salzburg would make the Archbishop laugh : such humiliation must at all costs be avoided. There had to be resplendent success in Vienna, Paris or London. Quite apart from the Archbishop, his Salzburg

K

friends and neighbours required impressing. However, Leopold was quite prepared to be sensible if something really solid were offered in places like Munich or Mannheim. But once in Mannheim, and one was on the Rhine. Over that river, and one was on the road to Paris, that capital of capitals which had before been so entranced by his children and in which surely anything might happen.

As this journey to Paris, the death of his mother, and his meeting with and later rejection by Aloysia Weber, together formed the turning point of his life, we have spent some time in sketching the points of view of the three most important members of the Mozart household involved. It is now our task to look at matters through the eyes of the Archbishop.

In the first place, he had very many other things to think about besides the Mozarts. Chief of these was the Bavarian question with its threat of invasion. The Elector was old, and it was known as far away as Paris that the Emperor himself had hoped to succeed to the Dukedom and indeed had married Bavaria's sister to this end. Succession to the Dukedom would incorporate Bavaria into the Hapsburg possessions, which would then lie both to the north and to the east of Salzburg. Colloredo must have wondered if he was to be the last sovereign of Salzburg. And suppose the Emperor succeeded in winning the true friendship of his brother-in-law, Louis XVI? Colloredo would know very well why the Emperor found it worth while to travel to Paris, visiting Salzburg en route. What Power would act as makeweight if the Hapsburgs bought off the French?

As to the Mozarts, it was to the Archbishop merely a question of whether a subordinate purveyor of one of his several amusements left his employment. A short Minute on a month-old letter : a Memorandum to brace morale : an angry look or exclamation if music held up the acceptable termination of High Mass : these moments of attention were all Colloredo could spare.

As for his Konzertmeister's compositions appealing in any special way because they were " aristocratic," Colloredo seems never to have recognised, much less sought out, this ingredient so obvious to modern ears. Wolfgang Mozart himself, with his half right by birth to minor aristocracy, was clearly less acceptable to the Archbishop than was the obvious peasant Joseph Haydn to Prince Esterhazy, or was the pushing Court servant Dittersdorf to the Bishop of Grosswardein. Had Colloredo noticed anything " aristocratic " in Wolfgang or in his music, we should not assume that he would have been pleased.

It was on 23rd September 1777 that mother and son left Salzburg for what afterwards proved to be an extended tour through Western Germany and a tragic stay in Paris.

# Intermezzo

## LEOPOLD, NANNERL AND BIMPERL ALONE

THE PLAN OF this book is to study the relationship between Mozart and Salzburg : we will therefore not follow the composer and his mother on their journey which was at length to take them as far as Paris, but remain behind in Salzburg to watch the father and sister in their Hannibalplatz house. Their landlady lived next door to their rented house, the new theatre was opposite, from their front door the bridge over the Salzach to the main city was to the left, and across the bridge Leopold Mozart would often have to go, visiting Cathedral, Residenz, Court, Archbishop, friends and enemies for rehearsals and for intrigue.

Leopold Mozart is one of the most clearly limned personages of the past who never themselves rose to great power, fortune or fame. He was never a Dr. Johnson in repute or in prestige, yet we know as much about his character and background. We know much more about him than we do about the diarist Evelyn. Fathers of great sons are usually shadowy figures, Leopold Mozart is unique in musical history, for the father of C. P. E. Bach is obviously ruled out. We confine ourselves to men not in themselves great. The nearest comparison is perhaps banker Mendelssohn, though he himself regretfully said that once he was the son of his father, and that now he was the father of his son. Leopold was the father of his son ever since that son had been 5.

Leopold and Nannerl said good-bye, and watched the coach with wife and brother rattle off from the Hannibalplatz : they could see the vehicle later on, as it proceeded on the other side of the river along the Innsbruck road where, at the boundary, it was held up for a quarter of an hour ᴹ²⁰. Leopold turned and climbed the steps to his front door when, suddenly recollecting he had not given his son a father's blessing, he ran indoors and upstairs to a window from whence he could see across the river to the town gates. At this date there were no buildings on either side of the Salzach between the Mirabell and the Innsbruck road. But he saw nothing of the coach, and concluding it had passed through, he sat down for a long time, feeling miserable. But his daughter claimed his attention : she seemed really ill and he made her lie down. He then went to his room to lie down himself, and slept. He was awoken by Bimperl, who came in to ask for a walk. So he got his fur coat and, seeing his daughter was asleep, went out alone with the dog. When he came back he ordered lunch from Thérèse the maid and woke Nannerl who, however, when it came could eat nothing. The faithful Abbé Bullinger called and prayed with Leopold, who continued in prayer after the Abbé had left. Then the two Mozarts began to cheer up little by little : they had a good supper together and played picquet.

Gradually things settled down : the shooting games started again, with the Abbé deputising for Frau Mozart. Nannerl went to Mass or gazed at the theatregoers out of the window. Leopold received his friends who remained closeted with him for hours while there was grave discussion whether mother and son should stay in this or that town. Leopold spent further hours at his writing desk, sending off letters to the travellers and also those financial calculations which either distracted his son or which taught him to ignore future ones altogether. He sent on many parcels. Some contained scores : K 185, 218, 219, 261, 269. Others were Leopold's fussing : a pair of trousers, some cloth for patching clothes, a steel button, a pair of his own stockings which he found too tight. A newly-painted portrait of Wolfgang was put in a conspicuous place for the admiration of visitors.

Bimperl never forgot the absent ones, and besides spending hours in watching, she was most disturbed when both Leopold and Nannerl were out together, fearing that they too had abandoned her. When she discovered her error each time on their return, she showed so much joy that she was unable to get her breath.

Salzburg's centre still lay across the Salzach, and Michael Haydn, for one, awaits discussion. But as I leave Leopold Mozart, my mind's eye has a clear picture of him at his desk. By his side is a list, to which he refers from time to time as he proceeds with a letter to his son. He has, for instance, already ticked the item on the list referring to boot trees. Wolfgang has been duly reminded to put them in his boots. Then, next, he must warn him yet again there must be no jokes about the Mufti in correspondence. Another tick. By now he is a little tired, and he takes from a drawer the last MS. he has received from Wolfgang. Page by page he turns it over, lost in love and in wonder, his bitterness and his worry alike forgotten.

## Michael Haydn

Michael Haydn was improving his position. His talents were by no means limited, even though his fame was obscured by his great brother and he was often rather sniffed at by the Mozarts. He was organist of St. Peter's and later of the Trinity Church as well. This church is in the Hannibalplatz, and Michael Haydn passed the Mozarts' house every time he went there. Nannerl too was a daily visitor to the same church, attending an early Mass to pray for her brother's success and, we must add, freedom from undesirable feminine entanglements, among whom she would have included her future sister-in-law, had she then known her.

Michael Haydn quarrelled with Kapellmeister Rust : at a rehearsal he asked Rust why he should be kept waiting for the Italian idiots who had not turned up " auf die Welschen Esel warten," at which Rust thought his authority impugned [M 20]. But the Archbishop was becoming very pleased with Michael Haydn's music, and clearly Rust could do nothing. On one occasion Colloredo, after hearing a Michael Haydn Mass, said he had not supposed Haydn could compose so well and " Bier nichts als Burgunder trinken," but Leopold says elsewhere that the Archbishop did little towards financing Haydn's desirable cellar of Burgundy. " Che generosità " exclaims Leopold sardonically when Colloredo gives Haydn six Bavarian thalers for incidental music to a play of his favourite French author, Voltaire. These thalers would be about equal to eighteen English shillings of 1777, or perhaps £5 to-day [A 10, M 19]. Further,

Rust was in ill health, and Dr. Barisani, Leopold's own doctor, said that Rust had better leave Salzburg if he did not wish to leave his bones there. So Haydn's position was doubly secure, in spite of his nominal superior. At one time Leopold Mozart even thought Michael Haydn might become Kapellmeister. In considering the tone of Leopold Mozart's remarks about Michael Haydn, we must remember that the womenfolk of the Mozart household disliked Haydn's wife, the singer born Lipp. But the two Mozart men respected the musician, and Wolfgang's friendliness to all necessarily included Michael Haydn.

### Ceccarelli

Another cause of general disturbance in musical circles in Salzburg was Rust's desire to push the fortunes of Ceccarelli, a castrato who first sang before the Archbishop on 26th October 1777. He was a tall thin Italian with a long face and low forehead, and Leopold liked neither his appearance nor his singing. Nevertheless, owing to Rust's advocacy, the Archbishop gave him a salary of 800 gulden a year for six years, a salary to be compared with Leopold's own meagre 240, though one supposes that Leopold diminished his own salary for rhetorical effect. However, we do know that he had to give lessons to augment it to a sufficient standard of maintenance for his family. A curiosity about Salzburg salaries is that when Wolfgang returned home after the Paris visit (which new period will be dealt with in the next chapter) and was made Cathedral organist in place of Adlgasser, he received 450 gulden, more than his own father himself said he was paid.

As for Ceccarelli's 800 a year, it can be taken for granted

that in any Italianate German Court in the eighteenth century an Italian castrato singer would command a greater salary than any other musician about the place. The same sort of thing happened in England when we consider the huge amounts paid by or for Handel to his opera castrati, though in England music masters and composers were looked after better than in Salzburg. The Duchess of Marlborough gave Bononcini £500 a year and George III gave J. C. Bach £300. Now, although the cost of living was higher in London than in Salzburg, it is clear that the salaried musician in London was far better off than his Salzburg equivalent with the nominal rate of exchange such that one pound sterling could buy ten gulden.

Ceccarelli put up in a wig maker's house at first, and then in that of a Master of Fence. But throughout his stay, he had his meals with Varesco, a Court Chaplain, the same man who was to write the libretto for *Idomeneo*.

Ceccarelli sang in K 275, a Missa Brevis in B flat, in the Cathedral. A lively account of a Haydn Mass earlier is given in one of Leopold's letters, and we may imagine something of the same state, ceremonial and lively fuss for this Mozart Mass with Ceccarelli singing this sort of thing.

Benedictus K 275 (Mass in B♭)

Be-ne-di-ctus,qui ve-nit in no - mi-ne Do-mi-ne
A♮6
5
E♭

## Death of Adlgasser

It seems to have been the afternoon of that same Sunday 21st December 1777 on which K 275 was sung that

Adlgasser, at the organ during Vespers, was seized by a fatal apoplectic fit.

This dramatic event drove Leopold to his writing desk to advise his son. He put on his most secret disposition : when von Firmian approached him officially on behalf of the Archbishop to sound him about his son being the next organist, Leopold played for time. Yet it was this very position which Wolfgang did in fact later occupy. Leopold successfully kept the position open, and it is due to this piece of diplomacy that Wolfgang had any position at all to fall back upon when his Paris adventure ended in such disappointment. It would not have been Leopold, nor perhaps would it have been Salzburg, if he had said plainly to von Firmian " My son is travelling in the hope of securing a better paid and more responsible appointment. However, he may fail in this attempt. Would it please be possible to keep the organist-ship open for him, for a year or two ? "

Leopold and his daughter did not live long alone in their house, for its master, who in certain moods was kind, and who was always religious, gave a room to a poor cap mender. Apart from that, its emptiness depressed him : he always half expected to hear his son playing when he opened the front door. But when he added two Italian male opera singers, his wife from abroad wrote to protest : would they not behave like swine, and spoil the stove by overforcing heat from it ? They did not stop long.

Then arose the question of taking in a pupil. Another letter from his wife, when she was in Munich, introduced the name of a Fräulein von Hamm : Leopold did not want an unteachable pupil who would do him no credit. He writes to his wife that she may test Fräulein von

Hamm by getting Wolfgang to play her a two-bar phrase and seeing if she can duplicate the rhythm.

But the Fräulein got herself out of this test by a mouse-like "Bravissimi" when Wolfgang had played the short phrase, and the whole thing became too much for his sense of humour. Then the von Hamms and the Mozarts differed on the question of money. Leopold wanted 200 gulden a year. Her father offered 25 kreutzer a day, which works out to 152 gulden a year if she never had a holiday. To Leopold's demand for 200 gulden there was no reply, and the matter dropped.

Adlgasser's death meant more to Leopold than that there might be an appointment for Wolfgang if he had, after all, to return from his tour without anything better. Adlgasser did things besides playing the organ in the Cathedral. There was, for instance, the musical tutorship of the Archbishop's nieces, daughters of Countess Lodron, for whom Wolfgang had already written the concerto for three harpsichords mentioned above, K 242. Eventually Leopold secured this appointment for himself, but not before the usual tortuous path had been trod. Countess Lodron was forced to ask him with a humility which Leopold branded as insincere. " I don't care if I do " was Leopold's warmest thanks, and this lack of charm hardly endeared Leopold further to the Countess's brother, who must have been sick of the name " Mozart " which greeted him wherever he turned.

*Rumours*

Rumours about how young Mozart was getting on in the Rhineland and in Paris began to circulate in Salzburg. His father welcomed them if they were likely to displease the Archbishop. Leopold took it for granted that

Colloredo would be spiteful, and therefore his greatest
hopes of wounding the Archbishop were when His
Grace heard the completely false rumour that both the
Mozarts, father as well as son, were to be appointed to
the Court of the Elector of Bavaria at a combined salary
of 1,600 gulden, about three times as much as their combined Salzburg salaries, when paid.

There is no suggestion that the Archbishop was either
spiteful or benignant : he may just have been bored. He
never made any vindictive move, now or later. The
Court officials were by no means in opposition to the
Mozarts. The Court Chamberlain, Count Arco, quite
openly took their side. He considered that Wolfgang
had been badly treated, and was rather pleased that
Adlgasser's death took the Cathedral authorities at a
disadvantage.     Leopold reproduces a conversation
between the Chamberlain and a canon of the Cathedral
in considerable detail ᴹ¹⁸. This is the only specific
case we know of, but the repeated rumours had human
mouths, or they would have ceased. It is clear that
Wolfgang's connections, offers and movements were
exaggerated and that they always made welcome news
in Salzburg.     Salzburgians were not surprised that
Wolfgang was received in foreign Courts, for there seems
to have been general acquiescence in the view that his
merits were above his present station, and, for a non-
Italian, were indeed exceptional.

Colloredo himself set the pro-Italian fashion, and had
himself implanted Leopold's bitterness. He was reported
to Leopold Mozart as saying that Wolfgang did not know
enough, and should go to one of the famous Conserva-
toires of Naples. This really humiliated Leopold, and
of course the remark, if ever made, was sheer nonsense.

Whatever Colloredo did say no doubt lost nothing in the telling.

Meanwhile the great Italian of Bologna was not forgotten in the Mozart household. A few days before the Christmas of 1777, Leopold Mozart wrote to Padre Martini to tell him that the portrait of his son which had hung in the Hannibalplatz home during the autumn was on its way to Bologna, c/o Haffners, which banking firm had, as we have seen, many other sides to it, and many foreign contacts. As, however, it is a copy, and not an original, which is now in the Liceo Musicale, Bologna, it may be that Leopold craftily sent Martini the copy and kept the original. It is too often found in biographies (Einstein p. 276 [E1], Anderson p. 432 [M18]) for it to be necessary as a present reproduction.

The letter which heralded the portrait was in parts graceful and touching. " I have only one merit : I really have tried to foster the talent which God has given my son." As, however, the portrait and the letter had to work for the good of the Mozarts, Leopold asks the great Martini, whose name was venerated throughout Europe, to write to the Elector Palatine about Wolfgang in case there was a good appointment vacant in Mannheim.

## War of the Bavarian Succession

This Elector had other things to think of. His ambition was to take over Bavaria, a Duchy which the Emperor was also claiming on the strength of being the deceased Duke's brother-in-law. Leopold Mozart watched with fascination : he loved the strife of kings. He had already been titillated by news from America. In Germany this was how the English were being

defeated by the Americans, but when Wolfgang was in
Paris, the news was how the English were being defeated
by the French. But now there was this Bavarian business,
nearer and sweeter. And what was this rumour which he
heard round Salzburg that if the Palatinate won, his
son would be the new Kapellmeister in Munich? He,
Leopold, makes a move in the direction of Bologna :
this sets in motion machinery which, acting through
Mannheim, returns to Salzburg bearing a Munich
rumour. Very pretty.

But, unfortunately, not true, for Padre Martini had
not written to the Elector at Mannheim after all. When
Leopold discovered this, he wrote again to Bologna,
quoting Martini's exact words of promise, a thing few
like.

As to his sentiments about the war, the Mozarts never
had much more than an anti-French feeling, an emotion
which became vocal and even angry only in the case of
Wolfgang. Otherwise, Leopold managed to be pro-
Hapsburg while at the same time and in another part of
his brain, he wanted the Palatine Elector to win to
enhance Wolfgang's chance of a job. Delay and confusion
caused Leopold to make the remark, so common in most
wars, about headquarters soldiers, Austrian officers
" liaising " in Salzburg, and so forth. In discovering
Leopold's real thoughts, the difficulty lies in the lightness
of his irony, while Wolfgang's was as hard, obvious and
biting as that of a lesser English poet in the circle of the
Earl of Burlington.

At last the Hapsburgs won : they occupied Munich,
and would have remained there had not Prussia taken a
hand, Frederick the Great having no intention of allowing the Hapsburgs' power to grow. King and Emperor

wrote each other letters full of polished irony, much more akin to that of Leopold Mozart than to that of Wolfgang, behind the façade of which their armies continued quietly to mobilise. A clash came in the summer, but the fighting, as usual, was far off in unhappy Bohemia, and had no worse effect upon musicians than the discomfort of Ditters von Dittersdorf who, in the service of the Prince-Bishop of Breslau, had to practise great skill in helping to preserve neutrality for his ecclesiastical principality. Dittersdorf's appointment was of the sort for which Leopold Mozart longed : it combined worldly power with a noble title and complete control of the music, a position in which it would have indeed been rich comedy to have watched Leopold Mozart cutting himself with his own keen edge of intrigue.

Salzburg managed much more easily than did Breslau. Although Salzburg's territories ran along those of the Hapsburg Austria and of Bavaria, luck, skill, and Colloredo's many influential relations enabled him to be easier and more dignified than his fellow Prince-Bishop.

## Leopold Mozart's Gloom

While these things were happening far off from the limited sphere of Cathedral, Residenz and Hannibalplatz, circumstances in the house in the last changed for the worse. During the winter of 1777–8, both father and sister became worried, especially the father. Wolfgang was getting out of hand. He remained in Mannheim, hoping for an appointment, instead of going on to Paris. Frau Mozart obviously gave way too much. Then Wolfgang was using up a great deal of money and earning very little : was this because he was spending too much time in pleasure ? The mounting expenses of the tour seem already to have absorbed Leopold's capital and to have placed him in debt. As he felt his position as Vice-Kapellmeister in Salzburg to be insecure owing to his friction with the Archbishop, debt was a very serious matter. Nannerl offered to lend her own savings made from her teaching. We have met with exaggerations in Leopold's letters before, through his stories of the patched stockings, the old dressing gown, not being able to afford to visit the theatre, are all touching enough.

All the pleasure in the Hannibalplatz house now was the inexpensive one of chamber music. Leopold played the violin and Nannerl realised the figured bass on the harpsichord. Their music was often borrowed from the Cathedral Library, and they played the violin and bass parts of many and many an old Mass. Nannerl stuck to this so that she would be better qualified to earn a living as an exponent of figured bass were her father to die. They seemed full of all sorts of forebodings.

Leopold's gloom was that of the planner for whom things simply will not come right. He imagined himself to be an excellent man at forethought and at taking care in advance and at arranging. He was also extremely religious. But although he constantly called upon his son to be a good Catholic, to eschew women and to save money, he never seems to have thought it possible that God might have different plans for his son than he himself had. The " either this or that would happen " hypothesis was always in Leopold's mind. For instance, either Wolfgang would die on a straw pallet in a garret waited upon by a penniless wife and surrounded by dirty and noisy children, or, he would die in ripe old age an honoured Kapellmeister of immortal renown. As usually happens in life, the reality was something different and unguessable. That the future could combine both visions, both the poverty, the early death, the careless wife, and also the immortal renown, could not possibly occur to him.

Almost frenzied by his inability at such a distance to impose his will on his wife and son, Leopold would have made himself quite ill had not from time to time a new score from that same son arrived. Forgetting for a few hours his worries, his threats (" you will be the death of me "), and his orders, he could relax, for here was more music from his dear and inimitable Wolfgang, the pride and joy of his life.

## Better News from Paris

Next year, in 1778, at last his wife and son really did reach Paris. In the spring weather he was cheerful. Now there was a chance for Wolfgang to succeed. Every bit of news was twisted and turned to see if it could help : even France's breach with England offered an opportunity for a new contact for his son. Louis had taken up the cause of what Leopold invariably termed " the thirteen American colonies," and though Leopold disliked the principles involved in the American insurrection, Wolfgang should certainly call on Dr. Benjamin Franklin.

At home, his modest and inexpensive evenings with his daughter churning out Cathedral music were varied with visits from Ceccarelli, for whom Nannerl played accompaniments, " like a first-rate Kapellmeister," and then the amiable castrato gave them both a good laugh when he tried to play second violin in a trio.

So much more cheerful indeed was Leopold now that he undertook the purely honorary and rather tedious task

L

of leading the second violins in an amateur orchestra
which met at the Lodrons every Sunday afternoon. In a
list of this orchestra sent to Wolfgang in a letter dated
April 1778, we find Lodrons, Robinigs and Andretters.
There were priests such as the Abbé Bullinger, courtiers
like Councillor Molk, students from the University,
musical schoolboys, and servants. Pure love of music
drew together this heterogeneous collection. Leopold
was by no means alone in accepting at the Lodrons a
position less than his talents would suggest, for Ceccarelli
himself, the primo uomo of all Salzburg, sat at the last
desk among the second violins until it was his turn to
sing. When he did so, Nannerl accompanied him on the
Egedacher harpsichord with its gilt legs [M18]. Here
as elsewhere the shadow of the Archbishop darkened the
scene : Nannerl was asked to play a concerto, but was
unable to use the better harpsichord which was tempo-
rarily in the possession of her hostess's brother,
Colloredo, who seems to have been occupied with interior
decoration in the main public hall of his Residence, a
hall which was to be the scene of the extinction of his
temporal powers in Napoleonic times. So rather than
play solo on the indifferent Egedacher, she refused.

News from Paris continued to hearten Leopold and
when he read that Wolfgang had a chance of securing
the position of the Versailles organist with eighty-three
louis d'or for six months' annual attendance, he advised
his son to accept. This pay was equivalent to 830
gulden, and as the work was by no means full time even
during the six months of activity and gave opportunities
for Wolfgang to increase his aristocratic teaching practice,
it seemed part of what might amount to quite a good
income. Leopold pointed out that this Versailles post

would not prevent Wolfgang composing secular music, and that such secular compositions could easily be introduced to the attention of the Austrian born Queen of France.

### Acting-Kapellmeister Leopold Mozart

In Salzburg the father continued to turn opportunities to account : he pieced together sections of old Masses of his son's for the consecration in the Cathedral of Colloredo's cousin as Archbishop of Olmuz, and even handled the ensuing gratuity which was to be distributed among the musicians. The eddying breezes of intrigue, indeed, were beginning to blow Leopold's way.

Countess Lutzow, for instance, paid secret visits to the house in the Hannibalplatz to be coached by Nannerl in Wolfgang's pianoforte concerto in C, K 246 ; the secrecy being so that her regular music master should not be offended. He was Spitzeder, an old friend of the Mozart family who was especially beloved by Wolfgang when he was a little boy. In the past he had been one of Leopold's intimate confidants. In particular he had been informed of Leopold's tergiversations about being so very ill in Milan, when in reality he had been hoping for an appointment with the Court of Tuscany.

Spitzeder had been a singer, but on the decline of his voice had taken to teaching the clavier. He was not much of a success at this, and had to take in lodgers. His house had become very much a centre for the Italian musicians who were constantly coming and going in Salzburg. The enmity of Spitzeder, once earned by Leopold, could do him damage at his most vulnerable point, that is, with the Italian faction who had the Archbishop's secure patronage and preference.

However true this all might be, nevertheless, the Countess Lutzow had to be taught K 246.

Leopold's position was strengthened by the difficulties the Archbishop was having in obtaining a new Kapellmeister. This delay retained Leopold as Acting-Kapellmeister, for Joseph Lolli continued ill. Indeed, it was just as difficult to replace Adlgasser. Lipp was such a poor accompanist that Ceccarelli would break off from singing to swear.

The Archbishop's own sister, Countess Lodron, began to negotiate for Wolfgang's return at 50 gulden a month. Competition from Michael Haydn was improbable. His amorous misdemeanours were taken seriously by the Abbot of St. Peter's, and Haydn was threatened with expulsion from the house the holy Foundation allotted for his use. It indeed appears from a letter written by Leopold on 11th June 1778 that while Salzburg was lax, one or two known misdemeanours meant no promotion, while three of them meant dismissal. Haydn had already scored two.

A pretty touch. Haydn's second child, so quickly baptized on the day she was born, was named Josepha: had Michael his great brother in mind?

Michael Haydn indeed, according to Leopold, was taking to drink. He was sometimes under its influence when at the organ during High Mass where, on the balcony among the musicians, he was not entirely out of sight and could not have been out of hearing of the Archbishop: as to whether he was out of the Archbishop's mind who still had the war of the Bavarian succession to worry about, we do not know. But we do know that others in the Cathedral thought Haydn may be ill, having heard equally stumbling notes on the morning of Adlgasser's apoplectic fit. This obvious need for Wolfgang to return and be the organist seems only to have increased Leopold's expert diplomacy and time gaining.

The Salzburg horizon continued to clear for Leopold in other ways besides the public demonstration of the manifest unfitness of Michael Haydn. Many Italian musicians were leaving Salzburg for other parts. The oboist Ferlendis and Kapellmeister Lolli had already done so, the first for another Court and the second for Heaven. Kapellmeister Rust, not an Italian but much in Leopold's way, sought better health elsewhere. Leopold acted as Kapellmeister and did so with a certain grim satisfaction, for it was the Archbishop's own order prohibiting travel which necessarily gave him this temporary elevation, and the considerable hope of it becoming permanent and confirmed. The position of the Salzburg Kapellmeisters was not a tidy one (in spite of ᴱ¹), and appears to have arisen from a series of decisions made necessary by Italian pride. Thus Lolli, although designated Kapellmeister, had always been paid the salary of a Vice.

## The Paris Tragedies

It was in this happier state of affairs that three blows fell upon Leopold Mozart. The first and greatest, though we cannot detect the degree of his suffering beneath his stoicism and his continued interest in such things as his son's career, music and the Mozart family finances, was given him by the Abbé Bullinger.

His good friend had called on Leopold and Nannerl for one of the usual shooting games, and when the other guests had departed, the Abbé took his host aside.

Leopold was already grave from the news contained in
a letter from his son. This was that his wife was unwell.
But the Abbé had to break to him the news of his wife's
death in Paris, for it was to the Abbé that Wolfgang
had written the truth which, with kindness and tact, he
had hidden from his father. The tragedy hidden within
this tragedy was that Leopold, having lost his wife, was
beginning to lose his son also. This Paris visit robbed
him of both, the one suddenly and the other gradually.

The second blow, and who can say this was not as
great, was that Fischietti was appointed Kapellmeister
with Leopold junior to him as Vice-Kapellmeister.
From this date, Leopold gave up hope of future preferment
for himself, and became dangerously over-
ambitious for his son in compensation.

And this leads to a third blow, which was that son's
slightly ignominious retreat or even dismissal from
Paris. The news of this came in a letter from the Baron
Grimm from the house in the rue d'Antin which he
shared with Madame d'Epinay, and in which Wolfgang
had been staying as a guest.

Grimm and Madame d'Epinay were once amiable to
Wolfgang, but had now changed, and this may have
been due to the jealousy of Gluck who in Paris was
overcoming Piccinni by weight of genius and who may
not have cared to find Mozart growing up beside him.
The cold, correct and worldly Grimm preferred Gluck,
who attracted others to Madame d'Epinay's luncheons,
to the erratic young man from Salzburg whose choice of
companions was not wholly wise. As for Madame
d'Epinay, her generosity, friendliness and confidential
manner masked a greed for power. It was no use trying
to dominate Wolfgang, even Aloysia Weber was not

able to do more than to cause him great distress. His own mother could not dominate him. And, in any case, he offered Madame d'Epinay less excitement than a Rousseau. ·

Wolfgang was unable to keep the initiative in this state of affairs. He was not able quietly to withdraw himself from a household in which he was beginning to be a nuisance. He had ignored his father's advice to insist upon paying for his hospitality, he had been a little careless with his money and now, almost without any, did wish to stay in Paris until his sonatas K 330–3 had been engraved.

## Wolfgang's Return

Thus when Wolfgang informed Grimm that he would leave the rue d'Antin and seek refuge elsewhere for a week or so, Grimm was aware this either meant someone else's hospitality and gossip within those walls, or poverty in an unseemly inn and even worse comment. He could have paid Wolfgang a salary for nominal duties, but correctly thought it less expensive to give the young man his passage back to Salzburg, and by the cheapest route. This route was the slowest, and therefore meant more meals and more nights staging, all of which made Wolfgang feel his poverty and his helplessness. This diligence journey from Paris was the cause of a breach between Grimm and the Mozart family which was never healed.

This series of blows tended to concentrate the father upon the son more than ever. The death of his wife and the failure of his son, his own disappointments as to the Kapellmeistership, did not diminish his taste for or reliance on intrigue. But his intrigue now was entirely for his son, and it was from the point of view of his son's career that he more than ever evaluated events.

The future hiding the breach which was to come, at first Leopold's efforts to direct and promote his son's interests and actions seemed partially successful. True, the Mannheim–Munich hopes came to nothing, but Wolfgang was on the way home. Leopold, judging from the letters of the outward journey, feared his son's entanglement with Aloysia Weber. He had recently written to Wolfgang in the most serious vein possible— possible, that is to say, to Leopold. For instance, he had pointed out that Aloysia Weber could not hope to earn 1,000 gulden a year, and that even at Munich 700 per annum would be the maximum. We know that Aloysia, thinking Wolfgang a bit of a failure, turned coldly away from him, and that Wolfgang came home to Salzburg as much afflicted by this as by his mother's death. But to the father, he returned as one free from entanglements, though when he dallied at Mannheim on his return journey from Paris the delay certainly made the father apprehensive. All the more joy that Wolfgang did not commit himself irrevocably.

While Wolfgang travelled east and south, his father had a cupboard with doors made for his son's room, accepted delivery of the advance luggage, checked the contents carefully, took Wolfgang's MSS. round to an engraver and prepared to publish, and told all Salzburg that his son was returning out of love for his father, and was taking up his duties as Cathedral organist, and was likely one day to succeed to the position of Kapell-meister. This was partly true, for the Archbishop really

did confirm the Cathedral appointment, naming a salary
of 500 gulden a year.

But when Wolfgang did at length arrive, his cousin
Thekla from Basle was with him in the coach. He had
picked her up in Munich : her vein of salacity seemed to
give him relief.

# 11

# The Eleventh Salzburg Period

## AFTER PARIS

*Residence :*    House in the Hannibalplatz
*Archbishop :*   Colloredo

WHEN THE COACH stopped in the Hannibalplatz, the two cousins, Wolfgang and Thekla Mozart, were greeted by Leopold. Thus begins the last full residential period of Wolfgang in Salzburg, which started on 17th January 1779 and continued until 6th November 1780. He then left, perhaps in company with the Robinigs, for a visit to Munich which turned into a much more dramatic visit to Vienna.

First of all, he had to be confirmed in his position as Court and Cathedral organist. As we have seen in the last chapter, through the father's careful and for once successful diplomacy, a situation had been created in which the Archbishop thought it wise to hint at Wolfgang one day becoming Kapellmeister, if he would put up with Adlgasser's place now. The Archbishop also let it be known that another foreign tour might be permitted. Thus Wolfgang secured an appointment which he did not want. And the salary, promised at 500, turned out to be 450 gulden per annum [D 1 and M 20].

Thekla, " The Basle " cousin, left early in May. The widower with his marriageable daughter and gifted son were alone.

Leopold Mozart commissioned a family portrait, which is here reproduced although it is found in several works M 19, E 1. It was painted by Johann Nepomuk de la Croce, and shows Leopold, looking worn, anxious and round-eyed, his dead wife peering down from a huge life-size medallion on the wall and the two living children Nannerl and Wolfgang. Nannerl has her hair dressed so enormously that her face looks insignificant, while Wolfgang in the background seems mousy. All three wear rich black, and they are ranged round a harpsichord with white sharps and black naturals in a room orna-mented with anonymous objets d'art. The whole thing is a little too grand to be true : but it is infinitely pathetic. The bereaved and bitter father, the constrained son, and the husband-seeking daughter, with the mother dead far from home, make us turn away our gaze until, moved by curiosity, we look again at the younger man. It is amazing. Consider that from the smooth brow, which we see under the small periwig, and above those reticent eyes, came the mental processes which captured and wrote down the two great works in E flat which give this Eleventh Period its grandeur.

The painter of all this, Nepomuk de Croce, was a Tyrolese, at this time in his forties. He was in his way an itinerant tradesman, trading in portraits. He painted on the average one subject per week, visiting town after town seeking work, not only in portrait painting, but for the Church, specialising in altar-pieces.

As the three living members of the Mozart family were difficult to assemble, this family portrait was delayed for months, and Croce busied himself elsewhere in Salzburg, having first been careful to start. Thus no other painter could do the work. And surely the painting is a very competent piece of work? Certainly it came from the hand of an extremely experienced, if perhaps not very sensitive, artist.

Looking a third time at Wolfgang in this portrait, we wonder at his emotional life. There is considerable evidence that he really loved Aloysia Weber. Her disdain of him during his passage through Mannheim on his way home robbed him of the object of his ardour, but that emotion, objectless, may have remained. He flirted in Salzburg, and some of his women friends took him seriously enough. He fell very easily into Constanza's lap later on in Vienna. Leopold disliked and distrusted all the Webers, Constanza as much as Aloysia, and the mother more than either.

This abortive love for Aloysia Weber may have made a greater mark on Mozart because of his early death. That is to say, the proportion of his days clouded over was the greater in that the total of them was smaller. Composers who lived past forty had time for their personalities to absorb the stresses of the past. Beethoven and his platonic relationships, Wagner and his Hollywood life taken so seriously by the participants of the tragicomedies, Bach and his two wives and twenty children, the bachelor Brahms visiting the underworld, Handel absorbed in money and music, Verdi with his great early tragedy but serene old age, all these composers had time to recover. Mozart was as resilient as any, much more so than some. But even if the thorn in his heart was there for no longer than was proper for a Trollope hero, it was there for a greater proportion of what was

only a short manhood lived in circumstances which
forbade his ever forgetting.

This Eleventh Period was not so productive as some
of its predecessors. If we ask of music that it should
survive, we mean that it should still be of use to us. It is
not only sheer merit which keeps a work " immortal "
(as the word is) but also its powers of adaptability to a
constantly changing musical scene. Thus a formal Mass
for a Cathedral in the eighteenth century has a lesser
chance of survival than a string quartet, because that
Church for whom Masses in the eighteenth century were
exclusively written has proscribed their use in the litur-
gical sense, and they may be offered only as concerts.
An illustration of this may be taken from the works of the
two Haydns. It is not only that Joseph was a greater
man than Michael, it is also, and just as much, that while
Joseph wrote accessible symphonies and string quartets
as well as Masses, Michael wrote Masses all the time, or
more or less all the time.

Let us list the " immortals " written in Salzburg.

Seventh Period—Colloredo's Enthronement
    *Exsultate, Jubilate*, K 165.
    Sonata for Piano Duet in D, K 381.
    Divertimento in D, K 131.

Eighth Period—The Italian Symphonist
  Andretter Wedding Music.
    Serenade in D, K 185.

Ninth Period—Keyboard Music
    Clavier Sonata in E flat, K 282.
    Clavier Sonata in G minor, K 312 (1st movement).
    Clavier Sonata in G major, K 283.
    Clavier Sonata in B flat, K 281.

Clavier Sonata in F, K 280.
Clavier Sonata in C, K 279.
Clavier Sonata in B flat, K 358 (four hands).
Piano Concerto in D, K 175.
Variations on a Minuet by Fischer for Harpsichord,
    K 179.
Symphony in C, K 200.
Symphony in A, K 201.
Bassoon Concerto, K 191.

Tenth Period—Hannibalplatz
    " Lodron " Concerto for three harpsichords, K 242.
    Divertimento in B flat, K 287.
    " Haffner " Serenade in D, K 250.
    Divertimento in D, K 251.
    Divertimento for Horn and Strings, K 247.
    Serenata Notturna in D, K 239.
    Serenade in D, K 204.
    Divertimento in B flat, K 254.
    Notturno in D, K 286.
    Violin Concerto in G, K 216.
    Violin Concerto in D, K 218.
    Violin Concerto in A, K 219.
    Piano Concerto in E flat, K 271.

Eleventh Period—After Paris
    Concerto for two pianos in E flat, K 365.
    Sinfonia Concertante, K 364.
    Divertimento in D, K 334.
    Serenade in D, K 320.
    Clavier Sonata in B flat, K 333.
    Symphony in G, K 318.
    Symphony in B flat, K 319.
    Symphony in C, K 338.

In number of "immortal" works this Eleventh Period takes third place to the Hannibalplatz and Keyboard periods, and even in "greatness" we cannot take the E flat Concerto for two pianos, the Sinfonia Concertante and the B flat Symphony as superior to the E flat solo Concerto, K 271, the three greatest violin concertos, the "Haffner" Serenade and the A major Symphony.

There is a tangible quality about Mozart's music—it seems immediate, tactile. Some of the greatest of composers do not possess this magic at all. Bach does not. His greatness lay in quite different spheres : he moves the heart as much as does Mozart, his music is among the profoundest—to me the profoundest—ever written by anyone. There are passages in the New Testament so inseparable from Bach's melodic lines, and these passages among the most salient, that they seem an integral part of Holy Writ. Yet it is Mozart who possesses the immediacy of expression.

Among the works written in Salzburg the present writer would choose for the quintessence of Mozartianism the A major Symphony, K 201 (Ninth Period), the E flat Concerto, K 271 (Tenth Period) and, from this Eleventh Period, two works, the E flat Concerto, K 365, for two pianos, and the Sinfonia Concertante perhaps above all.

Although the Eleventh Period shows a shorter list of "immortals," the list of mortals is about as long as in other periods, but was written in a shorter time. In particular there was a burst of church music, for the virtues of which St. Foix [W4] puts in an ingratiating plea "le chant emouvant et pur de Mozart." Writing from a Catholic country, it is not impossible, though difficult, to understand this point of view. It is perhaps a

limitation in Protestant education that " religious " music
is felt necessarily to be choral, and, as such, in one of two
categories. Either that is to say, it is choral music of a
simple and direct nature as in *Messiah* or *The Magic
Flute* (almost always felt to be " religious " by Protestant
listeners), or choral music of a polyphonic texture, as
in *Messiah*, *The Mass in B minor* and Mozart's half-
finished *Mass in C minor*, K 427, dealt with in this book
in the chapter occupied by the Last Period. Mozart
is felt in Protestant countries to be a religious composer
particularly in the emotional and polyphonic choruses
of his *Requiem* and in the hymn-like chants of the Priests
of Sarastro.

Of this Eleventh Period Church music the most
important is a Mass for the annual ceremony of the
Coronation of the Virgin in the church of St. Maria
Plain outside Salzburg and now reached by the little
electric railway. The Coronation was a pleasant piece
of ritualistic fuss inaugurated in the last year of Archbishop Firmian's reign and therefore recent enough in
its origin to be well in the lifetime of Leopold Mozart.
Eric Blom finds a foretaste of Fiordiligi in the *Kyrie* of
this Mass, K 317, and perhaps we all hear Countess
Almaviva in the *Agnus Dei*.

There is an impressive maestoso opening to the *Kyrie*.
The treatment of the " et incarnatus est," though necessi-
tated by the kneeling of the congregation, is nevertheless
executed in such a way as to leave Mozart's sincerity in
no doubt. Throughout the *Credo* a markedly symphonic
orchestral figure holds the long movement together.
The *Agnus Dei* is similar to *Dove sono* in more than the
melody : the long orchestral introduction, the repeated
notes on the horn, and the climax to an interrupted

cadence all prepare the mind for a solo soprano ending to a solo soprano aria, and the sudden intrusion of the tenor on the *Dona nobis pacem* shocks us. So the Countess, too, had a lover !

This is hearing things backwards, however. The congregation in the Maria Plain church were as innocent of *Figaro* as was at this time Mozart himself, but we, in this later generation, and in spite of summoning historical sense to our support, may indeed be excused if we mentally transport ourselves from church to opera house, until the choir entry almost immediately after the tenor's entry brings us quickly back again.

There are a few other pieces of church music besides this Maria Plain Coronation Mass which may occupy our attention for a moment.

From the *Benedictus* of a Mass in C, K 337, we have this:

Benedictus K337 (Mass in C)
Allegro non troppo

it has a bolder and rhythmically more vigorous a subject than Mozart is wont to use, and the smooth, splendid counterpoint leads to a typical homophonic cadence, so simple, so different from the grandiloquence of Handel or the subtle and rich harmonies of Bach in similar post-contrapuntal cadences, that we fall in love with it at first hearing out of sheer surprise.

A *Regina coeli*, K 276, contains a mysterious short passage of mainly homophonic interest with a mysterious,

M

delicate and graceful violin accompaniment : the sort of
thing we do find in Joseph Haydn, but not often in
Mozart.

Clarinets are included in the fully orchestrated score
of a Kyrie in D minor, K 341. This serious work for
four voices is very individual, for Mozart's particular
vein of counterpoint which runs so smoothly within its
harmonic framework as to sound like homophony
adds greatly to the mystery and gravity of the music.
As clarinets were first used in Salzburg in a Mass by
Mozart in the next period, it is thought that this Kyrie
was written with the Electoral Court in mind when, at
the end of this period, Mozart set out for Munich with
the beginning of the score of *Idomeneo*.

There were other Kyries, and also Vespers, written
during this time, but they have little except stylistic
interest. While some of the church music shows Mozart
not only as a great composer but as a devout Christian,
several of the works not here mentioned in detail show
him as lacking any feeling except pleasure in finesse and
in polish. There is interest for musicologists in following
Mozart's mind with regard to merely physical or literary
connotations—descend, ascend, crucifixion, and the like.
But there is never in Mozart the wealth of associative
detail which we find in J. S. Bach. *Come scoglio* shows
him as too aware of the dangers of the method, and his
laughter was ever near the surface.

In admiring these less successful religious works, we
meet with the greatest difficulties in the solos. It is
not a question of accusing Mozart of writing " opera-
tically " as though it were a sort of crime. How else was
the poor fellow to write ? It is merely that his operas
are all better known to us than his church music except

the *Requiem*, and this last and greatest work reminds us
of the most (to us) solemn of his operas. Otherwise,
when we hear the sort of writing which on the stage
means Countess Almaviva, we cannot help considering
the Mass " too operatic." In exactly the same way, if
the MS. of a genuine Metastasian three or five act opera
by J. S. Bach was found in an old trunk at Cothen, we
may be sure that to most people it would sound too like
the solos of the *Mass in B minor*, i.e., too solemn, too stiff,
too churchy. That would only be because we would listen
with the wrong ears.

All this is particularly difficult for anyone whose
childhood was passed in circles in which the S. S.
Wesley Anthem and the Bach Organ Voluntary were
" right," were the thing for Church, for Sunday, and so
forth. Once children get used to certain musical formulae
and styles for special occasions, it is very difficult later in
life to make sufficient adjustment to include the solo aria
of the eighteenth century into the category of the
religious. There is one great exception, and that is when
the most vigorous and fertile operatic genius of London
burst into oratorio carrying with him the complete
operatic aria. Why " How beautiful are the feet of them
that preach the gospel of peace " should strike us as
essentially religious, while the whole of *Exsultate*,
*Jubilate* should be obvious opera, would take perhaps a
whole volume to explain—and a volume not standing
next on the shelf to this simple study of Mozart in
Salzburg, either.

Many of these church works were written in C major,
and in K 329 we may find a link passing us easily from
them to his works for the Theatre. This K 329 is a
single movement sonata in C for organ and orchestra

with oboes, horns, trumpets and drums. It is one of the
last of the long series of Epistle sonatas, and stands out
from its companions with its passages for solo organ,
and a general amplitude of form and splendour of expression, the first of which qualities was hardly to the taste
of the Archbishop, and St. Foix suggests that K 329 was
used during the Coronation Mass in St. Maria Plain.

Not that there is any ascertainable link, except the key,
and this is to beg the question, for it is the C major
tonality which makes the St. Maria Plain connection
plausible, that, and the date of 1779. There is a splendour,
however, about this work in common time and a bright-
ness as of sunlight conveyed by the continual chatter of
the oboes which, with strokes on the drum, conveys the
atmosphere of a somewhat spiritualised Coronation
March. Yet this is much more than a March : the anti-
phonal writing for the oboes, a magical Mozartian touch
during the second subject in which the strings suddenly
diminish a conventional figure they had been playing,
and a strong development section make the sonata truly
symphonic. There are no repeats shown in the score :
no way of shortening : it surely could not have been for
the Cathedral.

K 328 is an Epistle sonata for strings and organ only,
with the organ part written out. K 337 is the only
Epistle sonata to have an organ part which is not only
fully written out but is marked to play solo as well.
Unfortunately the layout of the organ solo seems much
more suited to a pianoforte, and is as usual for manuals
only. It is as though Mozart had been thinking in terms
of the pianoforte concerto when he wrote K 337.

The secular spirit of these strong, vigorous overtures,
some to prelude a comedy, others for an imaginery Opera

seria (such a sonata is K 329) is in contrast to the Epistle and the Gospel which they join, and quickens the sensibilities of the worshippers rather than directs their thoughts.

To pass from the worst of this church music, the works here left anonymous, to the music for *Thamos*, is to pass from the trivial to the pretentious. To pass, however, from the Maestoso of the first of the two *Thamos* choruses of K 345 to the opening of the Symphony in C, K 338, is to pass from the pretentious to the successfully and completely grand, statuesque and noble, and to pass from this symphonic portal to that of the *Jupiter* itself is but a step. Mozart's " classical " art, if we take the *Jupiter* as its summit and as differentiated from his " romantic " art as perfected in the supreme G minor Symphony, would therefore seem to have its small beginnings in his Salzburg Church music. The second chorus from *Thamos* has the simplicity and some of the effectiveness of a number from *The Magic Flute*, an opera which unites both romantic and classical elements, and this music to *Thamos*, containing in its first chorus the seeds of the *Jupiter* and in its second a clear, calm hymn, is therefore of greater historical importance than much of his church music. Mozart had heard the later operas of Gluck in their French dress while he was in Paris, and much of what later flowers so gloriously showed its first shoots in the revised score of *Thamos*.

Besides *Thamos* there were other dramatic compositions during this period, but if we put *Zaide* and the start of *Idomeneo* on one side for a moment, and dismiss two German songs with mandolin accompaniment (K 349 and 351), and three other German songs on texts by J. T. Hermes as conspicuous among Mozart's works for their easy and pleasant dullness, we have three sonatas and the Serenade, K 320 between us and *Zaide* and *Idomeneo*. One of these is for organ and strings for Cathedral use, and has already been considered (K 329). The two remaining are both in B flat, and one is for solo pianoforte and the other is a sonata for pianoforte and violin.

The solo sonata, K 333, is indeed by far the most beautiful solo sonata which Mozart had written or was to write in Salzburg. It cannot, like its Salzburg predecessors, be made bearable or even interesting on an old square pianoforte, much less on a clavichord or harpsichord, but demands, in its long lyrical singing lines, the sustaining power of the treble register of a modern overstrung. There are two remarkable passages, both a denial of the galant, and both symptomatic of storm and stress within. One is in the slow movement just after the double bar when the bass continues with the 3/4 metre while the right hand has a clear 6/8, the harmony created by the cross rhythms being a restless system of suspensions and anticipations. The other example of a new style in Mozart's rapidly forming personality is the passage between the cadenzas in the last movement, which for boldness of imagination and richness of sound is more like that concerto style which the very presence of two written out candenzas signalises.

The second of these cadenzas is not so called, it is true, and moreover starts on a diminished seventh not on a chord of the six-four, but it leads into a last statement of the main theme as in many of the concertos.

There is a passage in the first movement of the great A minor Sonata, K 310, written in Paris, as rich and bold as that between the cadenzas of K 333, and this B flat

Sonata fits in better with those written in Paris than with those written in Salzburg. Indeed, two authorities [E 1] and [K 3] are of opinion it was written in Paris as well as the others, but there is sufficient reason in [W 4] for it to be considered in a book devoted to Salzburg. Although stylistically this B flat has Parisian affinities, it is Salzburgian in being longer, looser, less succinct, more tuneful, and with an introspective slow movement lacking any touch of the sublime. If it be thought that sublimity is equally absent from the Paris sonatas, we turn to the slow movement of the A minor, when for a few bars (the four after the repeat) we hear a premonition of the supreme slow movement of the quartet in G, K 387.

The Serenade, K 320, consists of two works. One is a two-movement concerto grosso, in which the concertante instruments are pairs of flutes, oboes and bassoons. This wood wind dominance is used for jovial Salzburgian effects, as in the Rondo when a lengthy coda recaptures us just when we feel the movement is coming to a close, while the main tunes of both this movement and the preceding one have all the elegance and give all the delight we expect from such garden music. Very different are the other five movements : graver, darker, more mysterious. If we consider them as a five-movement Symphony in D, a symphony with two minuets and trios, we will the more readily link the noble, vigorous and sinister first movement with the poignant Andantino, sad and weighty enough to be the slow movement of any symphony, and completely adequate to this first movement. An energetic minuet and trio, with a " post horn " coda maintains the interest and refreshes the heart : perhaps the finale of our imaginary symphony, which is the true finale of the whole serenade, shows that change of mood in the composer which in Vienna later on was to disappoint so often. Here, then, lies a temptation to disintegrate a Mozartian work into its separate movements, a temptation we surely all feel in some works of the K 400 or 500 enumeration, but which is less pressing as a rule in the Salzburgian epochs. After those slow movements in C minor of K 271 and K 364 full satisfaction may be felt in the concluding E flat Rondos, and both these movements have opening subjects not unrelated to this of the D minor slow movement of K 320. So early an instance of Mozart turning away from the sadness of things too easily prompts a biographical explanation : the sadness of Aloysia's lost love, the post horns and the coach wheels of the final stage to Salzburg with the Basle as companion, and, in the finale, the gay determination to be happy.

The symphony in G might be reserved for discussion when we come to *Zaide*. This leaves the symphony in B flat, K 319 next : not that there is very much to say about this delightful and short work. It is remarkable mainly for its use in its first movement development of the four notes which start the finale of the *Jupiter*, and for a finale which may have been fairy godmother to the equivalent movement of Beethoven's Eighth.

Last comes the Symphony in C, K 338, a magnificent work for all its slight dimensions. There is no minuet, and the other movements are fairly short. They embody within themselves, however, a superabundance of life : the haughty, martial first movement with its very exciting passages of arpeggaic imitation is an amazing contrast to the quiet ineffable beauty of the slow movement, and in the last of the three movements, Mozart displays in a 6/8 metre that grace (among others) which he has more than any other composer, the art of depicting a spiritual glee, free from any afterthought, full of ravishing melody and devoid of any suspicion of mere heartiness. Grace and gifts apart, he was able to write this sort of music because he did not consider his works as meant to embody religious or philosophical truths of the sort which make a meaning or a message out of the problems of life. He was one who accepted life as it came, and did not seek, except in his very last works, and possibly not even in these, to show any relationship which may or may not exist between sun and shower, joy and grief, life and death. Mozart was so much a man born for religion that he never once in his letters even repudiated a scientific or metaphysical thesis : he brushed such things aside as of no interest. The relationship between the soul and its creator was the lesson of his youth, and the meditation of his death bed.

In this utter nothingness of temporal things it would be infinitely absurd to consider causation and relation. Things come, as they come. Only, for Mozart, they come transmuted into ineffable and immortal music.

This indeed is the traditional view of Mozart, the view which caused the more scientific and agnostic of critics in the last century to prefer Beethoven or Bach. They admired composers who seemed to them to ponder and to consider. They thought Mozart just a little trivial compared with Brahms or with Wagner, because they did not understand his complete abasement (in the words he had himself set so often) before *Domine Deus, Rex caelestis, Deus Pater emnipotens*. He felt no need to write what Romantics and many Protestants consider a more fitting finale to the G minor quintet.

But these considerations are too weighty for this book,

for in his Salzburg daily life, Mozart showed little abasement : he was worldly and discontented. It is only when we look deepest into his greatest music, as yet unwritten, that we understand things which are usually so difficult to communicate in a Northern Protestant climate, where the instincts side with Martha against Mary ; and in which a Beethoven toiling through the night to grasp an elusive and consoling conclusion to an inward tumult seems so sympathetic a figure. We may all occasionally feel a different set of values fleetingly impinging upon us. But no sooner is this new perception felt, than the words with which to express it, and these words so near, vanish with the perception itself.

This digression, into which we were led by a consideration of the Symphony in C, K 338, leads us in turn to the Divertimento in D, K 334, written, it is thought, for the Robinigs. It contains two movements so well known and of such universal popularity that they may be heard anywhere, scraped out by the one fiddle of a theatre " orchestra " in the interval, or on the pier, or in the restaurant among the palm leaves. The third movement, a Minuet in D, is one of these, and the other is the laughing Rondo : a treatment of the same basic formula is to be found elsewhere in music, notably in the scherzo of the Piano Concerto in G minor of Saint Saens. But Mozart nowhere attempts to disguise its unpretentious simplicity, and is content to see for how long he can make the obvious attractive. There is sterner stuff, however, in this Divertimento than the two popular pieces of tea-time music. Several of the D minor variations, and the first trio of the minuet which immediately precedes the popular Rondo, could be placed in a very different category. The use of the horn is disappointing.

But now we may approach the two greatest of Salzburgian works, both for two solo instruments against full
orchestra. Both are in E flat : one is for two pianos, and
the other for violin and viola. It is a pity that we do not
know for whom these two double concertos were written :
it has been thought that K 365 was for the composer
himself and his sister Nannerl, and K 364 for local
Salzburg players, which supposition by no means rules
out the composer as one of the two string players, and
possibly Brunetti with him. Kolb, who played solo with
Count Czernin to please the Countess Lodron when
Mozart was in Paris, is an alternative favoured by St.
Foix.

It would be tidy and convenient if there were similarities between these two works for two soloists and
orchestra. But a greater similarity exists between the
concerto for violin and viola, called the Sinfonia Concertante, and the E flat solo Pianoforte Concerto, K 271,
especially as regards the two slow movements, both in
C minor. K 271 was to some extent the matrix of both
double concertos. If we compare the pianoforte works
K 271 and K 365, we may note similarities in the shape
of the first subjects, both divisible into two portions of
which both first portions emphasise the root triad, and
both latter portions move in conjunct motion. Both B
flat subjects in the two first movements share an easy
flow. While if we compare K 271 with the Sinfonia
Concertante, we note, not only the two C minor slow
movements, but the more than octave skips in the
pianoforte parts similar to those so very effective ones of
the violin and the viola.

One passage of great beauty in the Sinfonia Concertante looks forward to the A major Pianoforte Concerto,

K 488. Both slow movements end with a simple formula wonderfully exploited : tonic, mediant below, supertonic below (pause), submediant above, dominant above, leading note below, tonic.

A great contrast exists between the first movement of the Sinfonia Concertante and both the E flat pianoforte concertos just considered, or, come to that, to the A major work. Mozart, in all his pianoforte concertos is emotionally supple and changeable, but in all his violin concertos his mood is emotionally more severe, aloof and static. This makes his subjects less of a contrast to one another. In his pianoforte concertos he is less formal and the inner logic which drives a movement forward is hidden in instinctive depths : the surface alone is wayward.

As St. Foix points out, it was at this time that music for two solo instruments and orchestra was in the forefront of Mozart's mind, even at the expense of the usual single concerto. These double concertos are not therefore " sports " (in the language of the biologist) which makes us search for explanations. Indeed, the appearance of the solo Pianoforte Concerto in E flat, K 271, is the surprising event. For instance, the Serenade in D, K 320, written in August 1779, has the usual concerto movements interspersed : these form a sinfonia concertante for two flutes, two oboes and two bassoons. While in Paris he wrote a concerto for flute and harp. The arresting nature of the two E flat double concertos, K 364 and K 365, lies elsewhere, then, than their unusual combinations.

The viola melodies of the slow movement of the sinfonia concertante have an amazingly direct and passionate quality; a part of one is quoted in Example 10 in Chapter 8.

We may now return to the short symphony in G, K 318, in the form of an Italian overture, with an Allegro spiritoso in sonata form leading into a slow movement in the same key which in turn gives place to a passage of Mozartian drama which has its counterpart in the later operas. This dramatic poignancy leads into the second subject of the Allegro again with operatic effect, comedy breaking into the tears : the first subject is quoted and the movement ends with a coda long and decided enough for an audience expectantly to settle into their seats. And then, does the curtain rise to show Christian slaves singing in the garden of Sultan Soliman ?

For this symphony in G, K 318 may have been used as an overture to *Zaide*. It is almost too obvious to mention that the next German opera with a Turkish plot should also have an Italian overture with a slow middle section. But the similarity in the two symphonic overtures, to *Zaide* and to *Die Entfuhrung*, remains there : the slow movement of the G symphony has no connection with the opening air of the opera, nor has the G symphony the same airy lightness of the *Entfuhrung*, nor its sudden loud " Turkish " music.

*Zaide* was never finished. Its text was written by Schachtner, the composer's trumpeter friend, and the two worked away at it until the glad news came from Munich of a commission to write a new opera for the carnival of 1781. At last, something from the Elector of Bavaria, and indeed that particular Elector upon whom, so to speak, Leopold Mozart had put his shirt, the one who had kept his Duchy against the power of the Hapsburgs in the war (such as it was) of the Bavarian succession. So Mozart dropped Schachtner and the German language for the Abbé Varesco and Italian. The Abbé was Court Chaplain to the Archbishop, and of course was well known to the Mozarts, though not belonging to the same circle of friends.

Varesco's libretto was even less original than Schachtner's. If Schachtner was following the " Turkish " type of plot, a favourite all over Europe, and used by Dryden in London, Varesco adapted a classical myth of Idomeneus in Crete, and even this not from his own imagination as to detail and to dialogue, but directly from works by Crebillon and another which, with music by Campra, had been produced in the Opéra of the Palais Royal seventy years before. Varesco's Italian version of the French was to suffer much from the alterations of the composer. And when Mozart had finished, then Schachtner took a hand, and turned it into German.

The inception of *Idomeneo* was in Salzburg : its growth and fulfilment elsewhere. It was to get away from Salzburg that Mozart went to Munich. It was a great event, for it was the first time in his life he had ventured from home alone, and he was twenty-four.

Behind him he left a father even less happy than usual, for his sister was beginning to take wings of her own. She excited the attentions of many eligible Salzburg bachelors, and at the age of twenty-seven it is clear that she was a charming, attractive and cultured woman. Franz d'Yppold, a middle-aged man who looked after the education of the Court pages, sought her hand, and for a time Nannerl seems to have contemplated marriage and even a ménage in Vienna, but in the end she married another, von Berchthold zu Sonnenburg.

Leopold Mozart found comfort in his son's letters.

These were affectionate and often boisterous, for directly
the coach wheels started turning, Wolfgang recovered his
wonted spirits. The death of his mother was a blow from
which he seems fully to have recovered. He wrote
incessantly about the progress of *Idomeneo* and about his
suggestions to Varesco for the improvement of the
libretto. Leopold in turn reminded him to complete an
aria for Schikaneder's production of a Carlo Gozzi
comedy translated into German, for this impresario
had once more arrived with his troupe in Salzburg for
performances at the Theatre opposite Leopold Mozart's
house. The aria was in fact completed, and at the time
gave much pleasure when it was sung in the Theatre,
but the MS. has disappeared.

On 29th November, the death of Maria Theresa took
place. Leopold Mozart then became worried in case the
death of the Empress should stop operatic performances
in Munich, nominally still part of the Empire over which
Maria Theresa's consort and sons reigned in turn, in
spite of the little disagreement over Bavaria. However,
the Elector, feeling no doubt more Bavarian than
Imperial, decided to allow *Idomeneo* to continue its run.
Colloredo, quite as independent, but not smarting under
an attempt to steal his Principality, felt the occasion
needed some act of abnegation, cancelled an intended
visit to Vienna and went into formal mourning for three
months. In Vienna and elsewhere in the Hapsburg
dominions all theatres were shut. In Salzburg, where the
Archbishop thought he had done enough and allowed the
theatre to continue, Schikaneder stopped on. He continued to give performances in the Hannibalplatz theatre.
There was in any case only Munich to go to.

As for the Mozarts, as soon as their worry over

*Idomeneo* was relieved, they found that all the death of
Maria Theresa meant to them was that Leopold had to
rummage about for his son's black mourning suit, get it
mended, and sent off to Munich wrapped round two
trumpet mutes.

So life went on, and the chief news was the success of
*Idomeneo* in Munich. Everybody seemed excited and
moved by the splendid music which, members of the
orchestra declared after the first rehearsal, was not only
more beautiful than anything they had hitherto played,
but was original as well.

Leopold and Nannerl planned to visit Munich to
hear the opera, and Katherl Gilowsky, daughter of the
Councillor and one of Nannerl's closest friends, wanted
to come with them. But Leopold felt he might have to
pay for her, and managed to dodge the arrangement.
Nannerl got a new dress for the visit, which dress had of
course to be black. Frau von Robinig and other friends
were already in Munich : the Mozarts could take the
uncompleted score of *Zaide* to its creator, and Leopold
Mozart could get away from the Abbé Varesco, who was
being a nuisance. As the Archbishop's Chaplain, Varesco
could not himself get to Munich to tackle Wolfgang. He
was really angry when he found that the libretto, as
altered by the composer, was to be printed in Munich,
and he so far away from the child of his brain, unable to
protect his reputation, while a musician who declared
that in opera the words must be the obedient servant of
the music was able to do just as he pleased.

Leopold tried to pacify the Abbé, and absolutely
ordered his son to see that the little book of the opera
(libretto) was, when printed, exactly as the Abbé wrote it.
It would make no difference either to the score or to the

performance if this was done, and it would pacify an influential Salzburgian, even if he was a " peggio del Italiano vero."

As for the Archbishop, he stayed on in Salzburg, made no move to visit Munich for *Idomeneo*, and the only news about him is that his father, Prince Rudolf Colloredo, cut his finger at dessert.

However, towards the end of the winter of 1780–1, the Archbishop set out for Vienna after all. And this Vienna visit was to include the incident between himself and his Konzertmeister which altered the whole course of the life of the latter.

A small point about their relationship at this time. When writing from Munich to his father in Salzburg, Wolfgang addressed his letters

à Monsieur
Monsieur Leopold Mozart
maître de la Chapelle de S A R
l'Archévêque de et à
Salzbourg.

When abroad, Leopold Mozart had often been called what he was not, usually, out of mere politeness, as when a Lieut.-Commander is called Commander. That is to say, he was addressed as Kapellmeister Mozart. But in this case his own son was writing to him, and both believed that the Archbishop intercepted correspondence. Bravado ? A hint ?

Father and daughter left Salzburg on 25th January, 1781, and so for the moment pass out of this book. There is, in the phrase, " no one " in Salzburg. If the plan of this book were strictly followed there would be a decent blank page, as in *Tristram Shandy*. But it is convenient

N

to say this : in March Colloredo summoned Wolfgang
to him in Vienna. Wolfgang left Munich on 12th of
March and Leopold and Nannerl returned to Salzburg
two days later. Three days after their arrival they got
news from Wolfgang of his uncomfortable journey to
Vienna.

So by the end of March, 1781, the performances of
*Idomeneo* in Munich were a matter of history, Leopold and
Nannerl were back in their rented house in the Hannibalplatz, Schikaneder and his troupe had left the Theatre
opposite, and the period of Court mourning for the
death of Maria Theresa was over. Wolfgang was in
Vienna.

Leopold took into his house a brother and a sister,
children aged twelve and fourteen, in 1782. They
belonged to the Munich Opera Manager, Marchand.
Heinrich Marchand, the boy, studied violin and piano,
and Margarete singing and piano. Nannerl and Margarete
found companionship in each other : the one a woman,
and the other a girl. If we can take Wolfgang's pen
portrait of the Marchand family seriously, Heinrich
(inevitably " Hennerle ") was a most precocious boy in
other and less attractive studies than music, though
Wolfgang is sure that his father's, Leopold's, influence
will reform him.

With the Marchand additions to his household,
income and duties, Leopold was, however, far from
content. A certain misanthropy grew upon him and he
concentrated largely upon what he considered the moral
defects of his son in Vienna, how he would not do what
he was told (by Leopold), how he did not take enough
trouble to intrigue, was careless of the future unless

pressed by actual debts, and generally far too optimistic of easy success. Although he was as much moved as ever by evidences of his son's genius, he was moved just as much, and in a contrary direction, by his son's growing interest in Constanza Weber. When the score of what is now known as K 385, the " Haffner " symphony, reached Salzburg, he was so disarranged by his son's impending marriage that he could not for some days make himself open the parcel.

Wolfgang indeed even began to be careless of telling his father news of his compositions. For instance, he did not send *Die Entfuhrung* to Salzburg as soon as he might have done, and his father said that he knew only of the quality of his son's opera by the fact that it had run twenty nights.

The violent quarrel with Colloredo and the less personal but even more violent one with Count Karl Arco, are matters of Wolfgang's history in Vienna and so outside the scope of this book, though the notorious kick is the subject of an Appendix.

We have now reached the stage when there is only one more chapter to occupy us, for only once more did Wolfgang visit his native city. This last time he did not come alone, for he was accompanied by his wife, Frau Constanza Mozart, *née* Weber, and a baby.

# 12

# The Twelfth Salzburg Period

## THE LAST TIME

*Residence :*    in Vienna, but stopping at his father's house in the Hannibalplatz

*Archbishop :*  Colloredo

A GREAT CHANGE HAD taken place in Mozart's mind and spirit by the time he alighted with his wife, her baby boy, Raymund Leopold, in her arms, on the paving of the Hannibalplatz at the end of July, 1783.

The years in Vienna had seen him a free man, and a successful one as far as earning money was concerned. His marriage and his own temperament hardly enabled him to keep it.

Among his baggage was an uncompleted Mass in C minor, K 427, on which he was at work to commemorate his marriage.

The three of them were greeted by a cool and forbidding Leopold and by a charming but curious Nannerl, already being wooed by her future husband, Baron von Berchthold, the Warden of that St. Gilgen institution which her grandfather had administered.

Nor was Wolfgang himself much at ease : he really seems to have feared arrest by the Archbishop. In a bitter passage in one of his letters arranging the visit he says, in effect, that Colloredo, being a priest, is capable of anything.

The few summer months which Wolfgang and Constanza spent with father and sister showed nothing more important than the two duos, the one in G and the other in B flat, which were written to help Michael Haydn who was ill in his house on the slopes of the Festung. This act of good nature on Mozart's part towards the head of a family which those in the Hannibalplatz disliked, resulted in some extraordinary music. What makes the duos so remarkable, when compared for instance with those which Michael Haydn himself completed, is a fullness of suggested harmony by no means incomparable with the keyboard duets of J. S. Bach. There is a continual interest of texture amazing when the essentially melodic nature of the instruments is considered. We do, however, feel a little disappointment that there is no quintessence of the Sinfonia Concertante, because of the necessity of using the viola to serve as bass for the violin most of the time.

Canonic and other interwoven polyphonic passages of great vitality are not sufficient in themselves to give the viola part the sort of solo material in which it may have leisurely conversational interchange with the violin. Even when the violin has a melodic expression similar to the open humanity of the Sinfonia, as in the slow movement of the G major Duo, the viola has no equivalent answer.

Second to these fascinating duos, which were, after all, completed, come two torsos, *L'oca del Cairo* and the Mass in C minor, K 427. This Mass was started by Mozart before the January of the year 1783. It was written as a sort of spiritual sacrifice, a sublimation of that which was promised by Idomeneo when storm tossed, to be offered in solemnity to God when his marriage to Constanza had been accomplished.

When he and his wife with their little son arrived in Salzburg, the Mass was almost ready, only parts of the *Credo* and the whole of that smaller section, the *Agnus Dei*, remaining to be composed. For some reason they were never completed, but the gaps were filled from earlier Masses, and "tradition" [E1] has it that, with Constanza herself singing the soprano arias, and with the clarinets so recently introduced into Salzburg, this Mass was performed in August in St. Peter's, the church near the Cathedral and between it and the fortress wall, with Michael Haydn as organist. We may suppose Mozart's kindness in composing the two duos was met by equal kindness on Haydn's part in helping to secure performance of his Mass under the protection of the powerful Abbot and out of the jurisdiction of the Archbishop. As we have seen, this personal safety meant much to Wolfgang, though we have no evidence that he was in fact in danger of arrest, and what evidence there is about Colloredo's character points all the other way : whether out of disdain or out of magnanimity, he was not a persecutor. Leopold's position was not hurt. The fact that Wolfgang never received a formal discharge from Colloredo was as likely to be mere administrative incompetence as anything else.

This Mass in C minor, K 427, is notable for the soprano solos mentioned, especially the beautiful, long and various *Et incarnatus* with its written-out cadenza. This area comes after a *Credo* which runs to the *Et incarnatus* in one long sweep, with a general incongruous

Opening rhythm of the Credo of Mass in C minor
Allegro maestoso

effect of Monastatos and his fellow slaves owed to the
rhythm in the orchestra. Other notable features in this,
Mozart's greatest Mass setting, are the gloomy grandeur
of the eight-part G minor *Qui Tollis*, and the lithe and
heart-easing string melody which starts the quartet of
soloists in the *Benedictus*.

Allegro comodo

Some of the orchestral introductions are long and
important, quite as much so as in his later opera arias.

After this Mass had been sung in St. Peter's the visit
seems to have drifted on, rather than been enjoyed. Of
the unrecorded conversations none might have been
more interesting than those between Wolfgang Mozart
and the Abbé Varesco. This cleric, who had furnished
the much mutilated libretto for *Idomeneo*, and not a very
original libretto either, now had another idea. Mozart
spent hours of work on this new literary scheme, and
found himself involved in the task of getting a little
theatrical feeling into a story about how a man reached
his mistress through getting inside a goose. Mozart,

who thought the more comic an Italian libretto was the better, merely tried to make the idea acceptable to an audience. But the Abbé, in spite of his *Idomeneo* experience, would not give way to Mozart's ideas, whether dramatic or musical. Leopold Mozart attempted to keep the two opposing men together, but Wolfgang got bored with the intractable Abbé, and the score was never completed.

In December, the three visitors returned to Vienna, from whence letters became more independent and sometimes even pungent in tone. Wolfgang never visited his birth place again.

The Archbishop, who had not shown himself in any way during the visit, got Michael Haydn to make alterations after the Mozarts had left. This was probably not delicacy, but sheer indifference. Those organ and string sonatas, " epistle sonatas " which had helped forward the tedium of the Mass, were to be replaced by short vocal pieces to be composed by Michael Haydn.

Mozart in Salzburg : it is much more than Shakespeare in Stratford, more than Bach in Eisenach, more than Beethoven in Bonn. Yet it is not so very much. While the music he wrote in Salzburg is ample, varied and great enough to give its composer a place among the immortals, we may doubt whether it would be a very prominent place.

His name would be unknown to-day to the operatic stage, for *Idomeneo* was largely written in Munich, and even the little *Bastien and Bastienne*, kept alive by puppets, was a Vienna work.

The name of Mozart would have been equally unknown to the smaller concert halls, and the two violins, the viola and the 'cello would assemble to play Haydn or early Beethoven, but never Mozart.

It would be in the great concert hall that his name would still appear, mainly for three popular violin concertos and for the Sinfonia Concertante which gives so rare a chance to a solo violist. Perhaps the early pianoforte concertos would have a small place in repertoires, and two or three short symphonies would be useful. One feels that what would mainly keep alive the name of Mozart would be individual selected movements from the serenades and divertimenti, and these works, showing him as easy and as lengthy, would give no hint of the powerful, succinct, strenuous mind.

Yet if Salzburg does not contain Mozart and if it did not form him except as regards church music, yet there was much action and interaction between his genius and Salzburg society. This did produce those masterpieces we have named in this book, and we have tried to show the sort of life he in fact lived in his native city.

And at least Salzburg Cathedral had its enduring influence, to be traced as late as his death bed. The *Requiem* is a work for a Basilica, not for a Gothic Cathedral, much less any smaller building. It comes to life under a performance of clarity and precision, and diminishes in appeal when taken misterioso. Its mystery lies and is made manifest in its very clarity : clear, strong light, the great Nave, the wide, clear aisles, no transepts, no lantern, no elongated hidden Lady Chapel. Nothing but the great Dome, the upthrusting pillars and the large magnanimous rounded arches. Even London's St. Paul's is not quite Roman enough, while St. Stephen's in Vienna is out of the question. It was the Cathedral in Salzburg, Italianate, light, clear, in which he imagined all his Church works to be given. All of them are for the Great Occasion in the Great Church : even the shortest is in full dress. His works for other Churches, as St. Maria Plain, were for similitudes of the Cathedral, and the *Requiem* has its mystery in its excessive light.

# A Chapter After The Last

WITH MOZART'S LAST departure from Salzburg this book ends.

Leopold Mozart never became Kapellmeister: Lodovico Gatti was in 1783 imported to go over his head. Gatti was a good organist and clavierist whom Colloredo had been attempting to attract for the last five years.

The two Mozarts, father and daughter, remained in their rented house in the Hannibalplatz, with Michael Haydn passing and repassing in the square outside on his way to and from the Church at the end. Then, only a year after the visit of Wolfgang, Constanza and little Leopold, Nannerl got married.

She married in August 1784, Johann Baptist Reichs-freiherrn von Berchthold zu Sonnenburg, a member of the minor nobility who occupied the same house and enjoyed the same administrative appointment (Hofrast und Pfleger zu St. Gilgen) as had her own grandfather. So she left her father to live in St. Gilgen with her middle-aged husband. As Freifrau zu Sonnenburg she was revisited by the same portrait painter, Nepomuk de la Croce, who had painted the Mozart family group. Her husband died when she was nearly fifty, and she herself lived to be eighty, residing all the time in St. Gilgen S25.

Six months after his daughter had left the home empty,

Leopold in February 1785 paid a visit to his son in Vienna. He returned to his lonely house in April, and to judge from the ensuing letters, this visit did not heal the breach made clear yet intangible during his daughter-in-law's visit to Salzburg.

Just before he left for Vienna, *Die Entfuhrung* was performed several times in Salzburg under the direction of Michael Haydn. The Archbishop attended, and said afterwards, " Not at all bad " (" Es war wirklich nicht übel "). And he remained until nine o'clock at a later concert at which Leopold's pupil Heinrich Marchand played the solo part of the D minor pianoforte concerto, K 466, the score of which had recently reached Leopold from Vienna.

When the parcel arrived Leopold was feeling very bored : all that is lovable immediately returned when he found that music from his son. It was always the one reliable thing which kept father and son from drifting apart completely, for Leopold did love music, and his equal love of money and of security could never kill the more thriftless and unselfish passion.

But the father never really forgave the son for—something or other. What was it ? Partly, certainly, his marriage. When Nannerl married she parked her little son Leopold on his grandfather whenever it was convenient for her to do so. But Wolfgang was never allowed such liberties, and his children were not welcomed by their grandfather. Even when he asked point blank if Leopold would not look after the (by now) two children so that he and Constanza could make an extended professional tour, perhaps even as far as London, the grandfather was sarcastic, and refused without any attempt to be polite about it.

At the end of February 1787, Leopold had some interesting visitors. Mrs. Storace arrived in charge of a very Mozartian group of charming young people, carrying a letter of introduction from a Vienna Colloredo to the Archbishop of Salzburg. With her she had her daughter Nancy, aged 21, fresh from " creating " the part of Susanna the year before in Vienna. Another *Figaro* " creator," Michael Kelly the Irishman who sang Don Basilio, was with the party, and also Nancy's brother Stephen, and Thomas Attwood, an English pupil of Wolfgang's.

The Archbishop was gracious, and they sang at the Residenz. Leopold also did his duty : he had had word of their arrival immediately, and took them round Salzburg, using the whole of one morning. At midnight, at the end of a very strenuous day, he saw them all off on their way to Munich. " There were two carriages with four horses to each, and they were to be preceded at each stage of the journey by a courier to make advance arrangements for changing the horses, for they were travelling post. Heavens, what luggage they had ! "

This sight of Leopold in the gloom of the winter night as the coaches rattle off to Munich filled with buoyant and talented young people, is our last. He died three months later [M10], on 28th May 1787.

This limited, yet historically great and morally good man had worked all his life, had worried, counted his money, given good advice grimly, never been able to take life easily, was a widower, estranged from the son he loved. In his last years his pleasures were in the music of his son and in the affection of his daughter and his little grandson Leopold. His had been a grey life, not however without its periods of wild hope,

short triumphs and blessed once upon a time with many
years of happy felicity and the company of a delightful
young boy, his darling son Wolfgang.

That lasting monument of his, the *Violinschule*, was
reprinted in 1787, that is to say, the year of his death, by
Lotter of Augsburg : and we may say farewell in the
words of the new title page, to the " Hochfurstl. Salzburgischen Vice-Kapellmeisters."

Of the chief Salzburgian figures the Archbishop
remains to be mentioned. The French marched into his
Province in December 1800 [W1] and he escaped to
Vienna. In 1803, Salzburg became the seat of an ecclesi-
astical Metropolitan only with no sovereign powers.
In 1809 Salzburg was incorporated into Bavaria. In 1812
Colloredo died, the last of the long line of Prince Arch-
bishops.

It was on 11th February 1803, in Vienna, that he
signed a document of relinquishment. " We Hieronymus,
by the Grace of God, Imperial Prince and Archbishop
of Salzburg, Legate, and Primate of Germany . . ."
bade farewell, with some dignity, to his secular authority,
while making it clear that he retained his spiritual,
which, after all, was by no means negligible. However,
he never again lived in the Residenz, or even in the more
modest Palace which is still used by Archbishops on the
other side of the Cathedral [G10]. Nor did he help Salzburg financially, though he remained very rich and
his old subjects who were now his sheep were im-
poverished. He demanded all his rents just as if there
had been no war, and incurred a great deal of unpopu-
larity. " The absent are always in the wrong," but
Colloredo's absence was voluntary. No doubt imme-

diately after the change from secular rule it would have
been tactless and would have been misconstrued by the
Archduke of Tuscany (the Province's first secular master
before the Bavarian merger) if he had lived in Salzburg.
Yet he could have done so later, and certainly in 1805
when the Archduke himself left.  As Colloredo watched
the snow drifting among the houses of Vienna in the
winter of 1803, may we not indulge ourselves in imagin-
ing him grumbling to the effect that a mere Archbishopric with no secular power was an unfitting job for a
Colloredo ?  That if his subjects did not want him as a
ruler, why, those hungry sheep could look up and not
be fed spiritually, either.  He would look after himself,
his family and his money.  Before turning away from the
window a little dismally, he might conclude that he could
not return to a city where he once received the Emperor
himself as a fellow sovereign.

Michael Haydn remained on in Salzburg, playing the
organs of St. Peter's and of Holy Trinity, his position
not so much improved by the death of Leopold Mozart
as obscured by the new Kapellmeister, Luigi Gatti.

In January 1798, Michael Haydn, who had succeeded
to one of Leopold Mozart's minor posts, that of teacher
to the Cathedral choir boys, found among the new
entry a likeable and promising lad of 11 named Carl
Maria von Weber.  His father, an able violinist, three
adult step-sisters and a step-brother and his own younger
and ailing mother had all come to Salzburg as a travelling
theatrical company, bringing Carl Maria with them.  So
he went to the Cathedral Choir School while his father's
family troupe sank into bankruptcy.  His own mother
died that March, and in April he was taken away by his
father for a visit to Vienna, and did not return until May.

By the following November the whole family, Carl Maria with them, had left Salzburg for good. Michael Haydn could not in these circumstances do much for the boy, though a set of six fugues written under instruction was engraved by a father anxious to show a prodigy as amazing as that of Leopold Mozart: a project in which, as in almost everything else, he failed.

It would be pleasant to finish this book with a Mozart. We cannot do so by blood, but we may with a Mozart by marriage. Nannerl, that is to say, remained in St. Gilgen: her husband was executor of her father's Will. Leopold left enough for Wolfgang to receive 1,000 gulden. But this is by the way. Our narrative would have to end here had not Constanza Mozart, when widowed, taken in lodgers in Vienna. She belonged to a lodger-taking tradition, marrying the lodgers. Her sister had married a lodger. Her own first marriage, that with Wolfgang, was the result of her mother taking in single gentlemen.

George Nikolays von Nissen was a Dane in the minor diplomatic. He retired, and took his landlady, whom he had married and who was of course Constanza, to live in Salzburg. It was he who wished for this, for he had taken up the fascinating hobby of his wife's first husband's life and works. He started to collect material for a biography, which was published in 1828: *Biographie W. A. Mozarts*. While the Nissens were living in Salzburg in 1825 Schubert and Vogl passed through on a holiday: Vogl singing *The Lady of the Lake* songs, including the *Ave Maria*, with Schubert himself accompanying. There is no note that he visited the Nissens. He was more interested in Michael Haydn, for whose sake he inspected St. Peter's.

Nissen died shortly after this visit, leaving behind him a partly finished MS. Constanza had two clear duties : take in more lodgers, and finish the book by her second husband upon her first. Her lodgers proved to be firstly her younger sister Sophie and secondly that older sister Aloysia who had spurned Wolfgang's love so long ago in Munich, and whose husband was now dead.

Anyone feeling able to write a novel about Mozart might well start with these three old women living together in Salzburg. What extraordinary conversations they must have had : extraordinary that is to say, to us : normal enough to them. They were very much the sort of women whose conversation is mainly about men, and one of these men, taken by them as just a man, smaller than the average, distrait, convivial, able to work anywhere, apt to be jealous, a man with delicate features, fond of coarse jokes, a man from Salzburg, a professional musician who wrote one of these three elderly ladies some fitting coloratura arias, a funny man who wanted to marry her, to another a man who did marry her, confidential anecdotes between sisters, the third sister listening " really, dear, he actually . . ." was just a man among other husbands, lovers, professional musicians, lodgers. Is it not this view of Mozart which to us would make the conversation so remarkable ?

These three old women, very feminine, not too moral, badly brought up and probably rather dirty, lived on during the nineteenth century. Constanza herself lived until 1842.

o

# Appendix

## THE ARCOS AND THE KICK

EVERYONE KNOWS THAT Wolfgang was actually and literally kicked out by Count Arco from the Archbishop's Palace in Vienna. Almost everyone says " shame ". Shame indeed it is, and Mozart was very greatly upset. But to get the affair in perspective, to realise there is nothing similar about it to Mr. Benjamin Britten being kicked out of the portals of Broadcasting House, to realise, in short, that there was nothing so scandalously humiliating about it to all lovers of music that even at this time of day we need feel anger, it is necessary to go back a long way.

The kicker was Count Karl Arco. His father was Count Anton Arco, Chief Chamberlain to the Archbishop of Salzburg.

The Mozarts had long been intimates of the Arcos. Salzburg society was in a sense class conscious, without, however, much of the " don't play with those nasty common children, dear " of the English suburbs. While Leopold Mozart was always reasonably subservient to the Chief Chamberlain and his wife, with the children and the dependants of the Arco family the Mozarts were on free and easy terms. Karl, for instance, had a younger brother, named Leopold, who was not only a pupil of Leopold Mozart, but an old friend and playmate of Wolfgang's as well.

Karl Arco also had a sister : she had married a diplomatist and lived in Paris. When the Mozarts visited Paris in their first tour they were invited to stay.

The Abbé Bullinger, the Confessor to the Arcos, was an old and trusted friend of Leopold Mozart. He was chosen by Wolfgang out of the whole circle of friends to convey to his father the news of his mother's death when they were in Paris and his father, unaware, in Salzburg.

Rosalie Joli, " Sallerl," a chambermaid of the Arcos, was a great friend of both Nannerl and of Wolfgang.

This loose equality, ranging from the sons of the Arcos to the chambermaid, was one of the chief things which wounded Mozart when, given apartments in Colloredo's Palace in Vienna, he had to mess with the other musicians, Ceccarelli the castrato and Brunetti the violinist. He felt he should sit with Count Karl Arco, and that he was humiliated at being put on a lower plane than the brother of an old friend.

Count Karl Arco, for his part, felt that here was a friend of his brother's, someone he had himself known for years, and that he was being " difficult." His father's master, the Archbishop, a being too high above him to be criticised, required Mozart should do this and refrain from doing that. For some reason Mozart seemed to have gone off his head : he did not want to do this and did want to do that. And he kept on pestering him (Karl) to hand the Archbishop a letter of resignation ! The Archbishop might well take him at his word, and then where would he be ?

In short, we can sympathise with Karl Arco's exasperation and may understand that the notorious kick was that of an older cousin to a younger cousin,

something of that nature. The Count was 38, too old
by far for such foolery, Wolfgang was thirteen years
younger. All most undignified. But the episode had
nothing in common even with a modern official snub
from some Council or Department or Corporation.
Patronage has not been superseded, but it has left Archbishops and gone to large public corporations, who can
damage, sneer and injure just as mortally as any
Colloredo. The more things change, the more they are
the same. If there is no parallel between Count Karl's
kick and any conceivable modern situation, there is
plenty of similarity between Mozart's sending in four or
five letters to the Archbishop and obtaining no replies
at all, in wishing to remain in Vienna and being unable
to make his personal plans because of the silence of
Authority.

We surely should not blame Count Karl overmuch,
nor even his august master, who after all had many other
things to attend to. We should not consider that we of
the twentieth century do things any better. Every curt
refusal, every unfair review, every rejected MS., may
wound as much as Mozart was wounded, and he felt
wounded, not because he was in fact the greatest of
living and perhaps of all composers, but because he was a
creative artist. All creative artists suffer, not in order of
their merit, but equally. How to refuse without wounding amour propre is the study of all good publishers,
entrepreneurs and officials. It is perhaps a problem to
which there is no solution.

And if we do not blame the Archbishop or his household, should we blame Mozart himself? Of course not :
he longed for the musical life of a great city, and here he
was in Vienna. His whole genius was alive : his greatest

works were about to be written. He could not have returned to Salzburg in the train of Colloredo : he had to remain in Vienna.

Because no one behaved too badly, except Count Karl, it was no less a tragedy, and the tragedy lies in Mozart's really injured feelings, his fear of arrest if he revisited his native city and that complete estrangement from his patron which was started years back when his father began his naïve deceits in Milan, and a general waste of spirit. His father made matters worse : his letters to his son during the crisis were unduly influenced by Count Karl's letters home and his own sense of what was owed to The Powerful. Like his son, he underestimated the moral character of the Archbishop, who was clearly above spiteful revenge, and presumably never clearly understood what the row was about.

# Bibliography

A 1   ABERT, Hermann

             W. A. MOZART, Leipzig, 1919.

A 2   ACADEMIA SALISBURGENSIS

             Corona gratulatoria sue gratulationes SRI Principi Paridi e Comitibus Lodroni, 1681.

A 3             Die Matrikel der Universitat Salzburg, 1639–1810, 1933.

A 4             Gratulatio panegyrica . . . Guidobaldo ex Comitibus de Thun SRE Cardinal Arch. Salisburgensi, 1668.

A 5             Historia almae et archiepiscopalis Universitatis Salisburgensis, 1728.

A 6             Insula . . . Carolo ex Comitibus de . . . Liechtenstein, Salzburg, 1644.

A 7             Juvavi ter felix urna Maximilianus Gandolphus e Comitibus de Khuenburg Archiepiscopus Apostolicae Legatus SRI Princeps, 1668.

A 8             Splendor Lucis novae in coelo, 1753.

A 9   ANON      A Boy Musician, London, 1887.

A 10           An Account of the Sufferings of the Persecuted Protestants in the Archbishopric of Saltzburg, London, 1732.

A 11         A Further Account of the Sufferings, London, 1733.

A 12  ARNOLD, C. F.  Die Ausrottung des Protestantismus in Salzburg unter Erzbischof Firmian, 1900.

B 1  BAEDEKER    Austria, 1896.

B 2  BLOM, Eric    Mozart, London, 1935.

B 3  BORY, Robert   La vie et l'oeuvre de W. A. Mozart par Image, Geneva, 1947.

B 4  BOSCHOT, Adolphe
                 La Lumiere de Mozart, Paris, 1928.

C 1  CAMBRIDGE MODERN HISTORY

C 2  COXE, William  History of the House of Austria, London, 1817.

C 3  CROLLALANXA, G. B.
                 Das Adelsgeschlecht der Waldsee-Mels, Vienna, 1889.

D 1  DENKMALER DER TONKUNST IN BAYERN
                 1900–08.

D 2  DENT, E. J.    Mozart's Operas, London, 1947.

D 3  DITTERSDORF, Karl von
                 Autobiography, London, 1896.

E 1  EINSTEIN, Alfred
                 Mozart, London, 1946.

E 2             Two Missing Sonatas by Mozart, London, 1940.
                 *Music and Letters*, Vol. XXI, No. 1.

E 3             Kyrie, K 90, *Musical Quarterly*, Vol. XXXVII, No. 1, New York, 1951.

F 1  FARMER, Henry G.
                 New Mozartiana, Glasgow, 1935.

F 2    FIRMIAN, Leopold A. E.
                Primitiae Metropolitanae Jurisdic-
                tionis, Salzburg, 1728.

F 3    FUHRMANN, Hans
                Salzburg and its Churches, Vienna,
                1950.

G 1    GAERTNER, C.   Geschichte under Verfassung den
                Salzburgischen, Salzburg, 1802.

G 2    GESELLSCHAFT  FUR LANDESKUNDE
                Salzburg, 1898.

G 3    GHEON, Henri  In Search of Mozart, London, 1934.

G 4    GIRDLESTONE, C. M.
                Mozart's Piano Concertos, London,
                1948.

G 5    GOETHE, J. W. von
                Hermann und Dorothea, Leipzig,
                1798.

G 6    GROAG-BELMONTE, Caroloa
                Die Frauen im Leben Mozarts,
                Vienna, 1923.

G 7    GRAY, Cecil   Contingencies, London, 1947.

G 8    GEIRINGER, K.  Haydn, London, 1947.

G 9    GROHMAN, W. A. B.
                Tyrol, London, 1907.

G 10   GAERTNER, C.  Leben  Hieronymus  Coloredos,
                Salzburg, 1812.

H 1    HAUTHLAER, W.
                Salzburger Urkundenbuch, Salz-
                burg, 1889.

H 2    HOFFER, M.    Salzburg, Berlin, 1925.

H 3    HOLMES, Edward
                The Life of Mozart, London, 1845.

J 1    JAHN, Otto    Mozart, London, 1882.

K 1  KELLER, Otto  Wolfgang Amadeus Mozart : Bibliographie und Ikonographie, Berlin and Leipzig, 1927.

K 2  KURTZER  Begrif der zwischen Chur-Bayern, 1761.

K 3  KING, A. Hyatt Mozart's Piano Music in *The Music Review*, Vol. 5, No. 3, Cambridge, 1944.

K 4  KUNSTSAMMLER Der Gilhaper and Ranschburg, Leipzig, 1908.

L 1  LEITZMANN, Albert
       Wolfgang Amadeus Mozart. Berechte der Zeitgenossen, 1926.

L 2  LINDNER, P. P. Monasticon, Munich, 1907.

L 3  LUTHGEN, G. E. Die Plastik der Spatgotik in Salzburg, Salzburg, 1910.

M 1  MARTIN, Franz Die Regesten der Erzbischof und des Domkapitels von Salzburg, Salzburg, 1926.

M 2  Die Salzburg Residenz, Salzburg, 1929.

M 3  Ein Fuhrer burch seiner Geschichte und Kunst, Salzburg, 1923.

M 4  Erzbischof Wolf Dietrichs letzte Lebensjahre, Salzburg, 1910.

M 5  Erzbischof Wolf Dietrich von Salzburg und sein Mausoleum, Vienna, 1923.

M 6  Stift St. Peter in Salzburg. Osterreichische Kunstbucher, 1927.

M 7  MEISELS, Theodore F.
       Von Salzburg uns Salz-Kammergut, Salzburg, n.d.

M 8   MEURER, J.      Fuhrer durch Salzburg, Vienna, 1889.

M 9   MISSAE      Propriae cum Propriis Sanctorum, Salzburg, 1627.

M 10 MOZART, Leopold
     A Treatise on the Fundamental Principles of Violin Playing, trans. E. Knocker, Oxford, 1948.

M 11      Drei Divertimenti, 1931.

M 12      Konzert in D, Leipzig, 1931.

M 13      Notenbuch, 1924.

M 14      Notenbuch fur Wolfgang, 1939.

M 15      Sinfonia di caccia, 1935.

M 16      Briefe an seine Tochter, Salzburg, 1936.

M 17      Traduction complète. Henri de Curzon, 1888.

M 18 MOZART, Wolfgang
     Die Briefe W. A. Mozart's und seiner Familie, 5 vols., Munich and Leipzig, 1914.

M 19      Letters of Mozart and his family, trans. Emily Anderson, Macmillan, London, 1938.

M 20      Briefe, 5 vols., Mozarteum, Salzburg, 1942.

M 21      Symphony in G, KA 293, No. 53 of E. Donajowski's 8vo Chamber Music, 1904.

M 22      Mozart Museum. Katalog des Mozart-Museums, Salzburg, 1898.

M 23 MOZARTEUM      Dom-Musik-Verein, Salzburg, 1841.

M 24                Dreiunddreissigster Jahresbericht der . . . Internationalem Stiftung, Salzburg, 1914.

M 25                Mitteilungen, Salzburg, 1918.

M 26 MULLER, Erich H.

Briefe Wolfgang Amadeus Mozarts : also M 20.

M 27 MANSFIELD, Orlando A.

Mozart's Organ Sonatas, *Musical Quarterly*, Vol. VIII, No. 4, New York, 1922.

N 1 NISSEN, Georg Nikolaus von

Biographie W. A. Mozarts, 1828.

P 1   PERTZ          Monumenta Germaniae Historica, Hanover, 1851.

P 2   PRETZELL, Lothar

Salzburger Barockplastik, Berlin, 1935.

P 3   PUCCETTI, P. M.

Vita del Cardinal L. Colloredo, 1738.

R 1   RANKE, Leopold von

The History of the Popes, 3 vols., Bell, London, 1913.

R 2   RICHTER, Eduard

Das Herzogtum Salzburg, 1881.

R 3   ROLL, Karl     Die Salzburger Munzmerkung vom Jahre 1681, Salzburg, 1910.

R 4   ROSENTHAL, Karl August

Zur Stilistik der Salzburger Kirchenmusik von 1601–1730, Vienna, 1930.

S 1    SAINT-FOIX, G. de
                        The Symphonies of Mozart, trans.
                        Leslie Orrey, Dobson, London,
                        1947.
S 2    SALZBURG         Brevis Historia de origine, 1661.
S 3                     Conspectus et status totius Arch-
                        Dioecesis Salisburgensis, 1772.
S 4                     Conspectus seu status . . . eccle-
                        siasticus, 1796.
S 5                     Cronia des Hochberumbten Stiffts
                        zu Saltzburg, 1520.
S 6                     Chronicon Salzburgense, 1728.
S 7                     Chronicon Salzburgense, 1743.
S 8                     Chronicon Salzburgense, 1495, 1743.
S 9                     Constitutiones et decreta, 1574.
S 10                    Domstift Archiv fur Kunde Oster-
                        reichischer Geschichts-Quellen Bd
                        28, Vienna, 1848.
S 11                    Fremdenfuhrer, Salzburg, 1865.
S 12                    Geographic von Salzburg, 1796.
S 13                    Handlung der Erzbischofs.
S 14                    Hochschulverein : Die Salzburger
                        Culterkampf, 1904
S 15                    Museum     Carolino—Augusteum
                        Juvavum, 1929.
S 16                    Reise durch das Erzstift Salzburg,
                        1796.
S 17                    Ruhepunkte auf meinen Reisen
                        durch das Salzburgische, 1806.
S 18                    Saecularis Memoriae defunctorum,
                        sive compendium vitae . . . 1782.
S 19                    Series ac successio Salisburgensium,
                        1682.

S 20                  Statuta Provincialia, 1491.

S 21                  Thranen und Seufzer uber der Kelch-Raub, 1732.

S 22 SALZBURGER INSTITUT FUR RELIGIOSE VOLKSUNDE Geistliches Volksschauspiel im hande Salzburg, 1936.

S 23 SCHNEIDER      Constantin Die Oratorieri und Schuldramen Anton Cajetan Adlgassers " Studien zur Musikwissenschaft," Vienna, 1931.

S 24                  Constantin Geschichte der Musik in Salzburg, Salzburg, 1935.

S 25 SCHURIG, Arthur
                 Wolfgang Amadeus Mozart, 2 vols., 2nd edition, 1923.

S 26 STROHSCHNEIDER, J. S.
                 Salzburger Mozartbuchlein, 1914.

S 27 SCHIEDERMAIR, Ludwig
                 Die Briefe W. A. Mozarts, 5 vols. : also see M 18.

S 28 SEIFFERT, Max Drei Divertimenti (Leopold Mozart), Leipzig.

S 29 SOMERSET, H. V. F.
                 The Habsburg Emperors as Musicians (*Music and Letters*, XXX/3), London, 1949.

T 1 TENSCHERT, Roland
                 Mozart, Ein Kunstlerleben in Bildern und Dokumentzen, 1931.

T 2 TIETZE, H.      Die Kirchlichen Denkmale der Stadt Salzburg, Vienna, 1912.

T 3                  Die Profanen Denkmale der Stadt Salzburg, Vienna, 1914.

W 1   WAGNER, K. O. Alt Salzburg, Vienna, n.d.

W 2                 Das Salzburger Hoftheater, 1775–
                1805, Salzburg, 1910.

W 3   WOLFENBUTTELER PALIMPSEST
                Salzburg Missal, 1936.

W 4   WYZEWA ET ST. FOIX
                Mozart, 3 vols., Paris, 1912, etc.

Z 1   ZEICHNUNGEN AUF EINER REISE VON WIEN, 1800.

Z 2   ZEITSCHRIFT DES HISTORISCHEN VEREINS FUR
      SCHWABEN      (A Buff. Mozarts Jahr: viii Augs-
                burger Vorfahren), 1891.

# Discography

K 271    Pianoforte Concerto in E flat, PARLOPHONE R
         20570–3 (78).

K 281    Pianoforte Sonata in B flat, DECCA LXT 2666
         (33).

K 283    Pianoforte Sonata in G, DECCA LXT 2666 (33).

K 314    Oboe Concerto in C, H.M.V. C 3954–5 (78).

K 318    Symphony in G, DECCA K 2200 (78).

K 319    Symphony in B flat, DECCA AK 1249–51 (78).

K 320    Serenade in D, DECCA LXT 2671 (33).

K 327    Epistle Sonata in C, NIXA SPLP 534 (33).

K 333    Pianoforte Sonata in B flat, PARLOPHONE R
         2056–7 (78).

K 338    Symphony in C, DECCA LXT 2614 (33).

K 366    Idomeneo, NIXA HLP 2020–1–4 (33).

K 423    Duo in G, DECCA K 910–12 (78).

K 424    Duo in B flat, DECCA K 910–12 (78).

# INDEX

P

# INDEX OF MUSIC

Arranged under Köchel numbers